JOAN OF ARC

JOAN OF ARC

Susan Banfield

Burke Publishing Company Limited
LONDON ⋆ TORONTO ⋆ NEW YORK

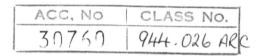
First published in the United States of America 1985
© 1985 by Chelsea House Publishers,
a division of Chelsea House Educational Communications, Inc.
Introduction copyright © 1985 by Arthur M. Schlesinger, jr.

This edition first published 1988
New material in this edition
© Burke Publishing Company Limited 1988

Acknowledgements
The Author and Publishers are grateful to the following organizations for
permission to reproduce copyright illustrations in this book:
   The Bettmann Archive, the Mansell Collection and New York Public
   Library.

CIP data
Banfield, Susan
   Joan of Arc. — (World leaders: past and present)
   1. France. Joan of Arc, Saint — Biographies
   I. Title
   944'.026'0924

ISBN 0 222 01201 3 Hardbound
ISBN 0 222 01221 8 Paperback

Burke Publishing Company Limited
Pegasus House, 116–120 Golden Lane, London EC1Y 0TL, England
Printed in England by Purnell Book Production Limited.

CONTENTS

On Leadership   7
1. A Prophecy Fulfilled   13
2. Setting Out   25
3. The Great Victory   35
4. A True King at Last   49
5. Dark Clouds Gather   57
6. The Maid on Trial   79
7. The Stake and Afterwards   95
Further Reading   108
Chronology   109
Index   110

WORLD LEADERS   PAST AND PRESENT

Konrad Adenauer	Ferdinand and Isabella	Mao Tse Tung
Alexander the Great	Franco	Mary, Queen of Scots
Mark Antony	Frederick the Great	Golda Meir
King Arthur	Indira Gandhi	Metternich
Kemal Atatürk	Mohandas K. Gandhi	Benito Mussolini
Clement Attlee	Garibaldi	Napoleon
Menachem Begin	Genghis Khan	Jamal Nasser
David Ben Gurion	Gladstone	Jawalharlal Nehru
Bismarck	Dag Hammarskjöld	Nero
Léon Blum	Henry VIII	Nicholas II
Símon Bolívar	Henry of Navarre	Richard Nixon
Cesare Borgia	Hindenburg	Kwame Nkrumah
Willy Brandt	Adolf Hitler	Pericles
Leonid Brezhnev	Ho Chi Minh	Juan Perón
Julius Ceasar	King Hussein	Muammar Qaddafi
Calvin	Ivan the Terrible	Robespierre
Fidel Castro	Andrew Jackson	Eleanor Roosevelt
Catherine the Great	Thomas Jefferson	Franklin D. Roosevelt
Charlemagne	Joan of Arc	Theodore Roosevelt
Chiang Kai-Shek	Pope John XXIII	Anwar Sadat
Chou En-Lai	Lyndon Johnson	Sun Yat-Sen
Winston Churchill	Benito Juárez	Joseph Stalin
Clemenceau	John F. Kennedy	Tamerlane
Cleopatra	Jomo Kenyatta	Margaret Thatcher
Cortes	Ayatollah Khomeini	Iosif Tito
Cromwell	Nikita Khrushchev	Leon Trotsky
Danton	Martin Luther King	Pierre Trudeau
Charles De Gaulle	Henry Kissinger	Harry S. Truman
De Valera	Vladimir Lenin	Queen Victoria
Disraeli	Abraham Lincoln	George Washington
Dwight D. Eisenhower	Lloyd George	Chaim Weizmann
Eleanor of Aquitaine	Louis XIV	Woodrow Wilson
Queen Elizabeth I	Martin Luther	Xerxes
	Judas Maccabeus	

ON LEADERSHIP

Arthur M. Schlesinger, jr.

LEADERSHIP, it may be said, is really what makes the world go round. Love no doubt smooths the passage; but love is a private transaction between consenting adults. Leadership is a public transaction with history. The idea of leadership affirms the capacity of individuals to move, inspire and mobilize masses of people so that they act together in pursuit of an end. Sometimes leadership serves good purposes, sometimes bad; but whether the end is benign or evil, great leaders are those men and women who leave their personal stamp on history.

Now, the very concept of leadership implies the proposition that individuals can make a difference. This proposition has never been universally accepted. From classical times to the present day, eminent thinkers have regarded individuals as no more than the agents and pawns of larger forces, whether the gods and goddesses of the ancient world or, in the modern era, race, class, nation, the dialectic, the will of the people, the spirit of the times, history itself. Against such forces, the individual dwindles into insignificance.

So contends the thesis of historical determinism. Tolstoy's great novel *War and Peace* offers a famous statement of the case. Why, Tolstoy asked, did millions of men in the Napoleonic wars, denying their human feelings and their common sense, move back and forth across Europe slaughtering their fellows? "The war," Tolstoy answered, "was bound to happen simply because it was bound to happen." All prior history predetermined it. As for leaders, they, Tolstoy said, "are but the labels that serve to give a name to an end and, like labels, they have the least possible connection with the event." The greater the leader, "the more conspicuous the inevitability and the predestination of every act he commits." The leader, said Tolstoy, is "the slave of history".

Determinism takes many forms. Marxism is the determinism of class, Nazism the determinism of race. But the idea of men and women as the slaves of history runs athwart the deepest human instincts. Rigid determinism abolishes the idea of human freedom—the assumption of free choice that underlies every move we make, every word we speak, every thought we think. It abolishes the idea of human responsibility, since it is manifestly unfair to reward or punish people for actions that are by definition beyond their control. No one can live consistently by any deterministic creed. The Marxist states prove this themselves by their extreme susceptibility to the cult of leadership.

More than that, history refutes the idea that individuals make no difference. In December 1931 a British politician crossing Park Avenue in New York City between 76th and 77th Streets around ten-thirty at night looked in the wrong direction and was knocked down by a speeding car—a moment, he later recalled, of a man aghast, a world aglare: "I do not understand why I was not broken like an eggshell or squashed like a gooseberry." Fourteen months later an American politician, sitting in an open car in Miami, Florida, was fired on by an assassin; the man beside him was hit. Those who believe that individuals make no difference to history might well ponder whether the next two decades would have been the same, had Mario Contasini's car killed Winston Churchill in 1931 and had Giuseppe Zangara's bullet killed Franklin Roosevelt in 1933. Suppose, in addition, that Adolf Hitler had been killed in the street fighting during the Munich *Putsch* of 1923 and that Lenin had died of typhus during the First World War. What would the 20th century be like now?

For better or for worse, individuals do make a difference. "The notion that a people can run itself and its affairs anonymously," wrote the philosopher William James, "is now well known to be the silliest of absurdities. Mankind does nothing save through initiatives on the part of inventors, great or small, and imitation by the rest of us—these are the sole factors in human progress. Individuals of genius show the way, and set the patterns, which common people then adopt and follow."

Leadership, James suggests, means leadership in thought as well as in action. In the long run, leaders in thought may well make the greater difference to the world. But, as Woodrow Wilson once said, "Those only are leaders of men, in the general eye, who lead in action . . . It is at their hands that new thought gets its translation into the crude language of deeds." Leaders in thought often invent in solitude and obscurity, leaving to later generations the tasks of imitation. Leaders in action—the leaders portrayed in this series—have to be effective in their own time.

And they cannot be effective by themselves. They must act in response to the rhythms of their age. Their genius must be adapted, in a phrase of William James's, "to the receptivities of the moment". Leaders are useless without followers. "There goes the mob," said the French politician hearing a clamour in the streets. "I am their leader. I must follow them." Great leaders turn the inchoate emotions of the mob to purposes of their own. They seize on the opportunities of their time, the hopes, fears, frustrations, crises, potentialities. They succeed when events have prepared the way for them, when the community is waiting to be aroused, when they can provide the clarifying and organizing ideas. Leadership ignites the circuit between the individual and the mass and thereby alters history. It may alter history for better or for worse. Leaders have been responsible for the most extravagant follies and most monstrous crimes that have beset suffering humanity. They have also been vital in such gains as humanity has made in individual freedom, religious and racial tolerance, social justice and respect for human rights.

There is no sure way to tell in advance who is going to lead for good and who for evil. But a glance at the gallery of men and women in *World Leaders—Past and Present* suggests some useful tests.

One test is this: do leaders lead by force or by persuasion? By command or by consent? Through most of history leadership was exercised by the divine right of authority. The duty of followers was to defer and to obey. *"Their's not to reason why,/Their's but to do and die."* On occasion, as with the so-called "enlightened despots" of the 18th century in Europe, absolutist leadership was animated by humane purposes. More often, absolutism nourished the passion for domination, land, gold and conquest and resulted in tyranny.

The great revolution of modern times has been the revolution of equality. The idea that all people should be equal in their legal condition has undermined the old structures of authority, hierarchy and deference. The revolution of equality has had two contrary effects on the nature of leadership. For equality, as Alexis de Tocqueville pointed out in his great study *Democracy in America*, might mean equality in servitude as well as equality in freedom.

"I know of only two methods of establishing equality in the political world," Tocqueville wrote. "Rights must be given to every citizen, or none at all to anyone . . . save one, who is the master of all." There was no middle ground "between the sovereignty of all and the absolute power of one man". In his astonishing prediction of 20th-century totalitarian dictatorship, Tocqueville explained how the revolution of equality could lead to the *Führerprinzip* and more terrible absolutism than the world had ever known.

But when rights are given to every citizen and the sovereignty of all is established, the problem of leadership takes a new form, becomes more exacting than ever before. It is easy to issue commands and enforce them by the rope and the stake, the concentration camp and the *gulag.* It is much harder to use argument and achievement to overcome opposition and win consent. The Founding Fathers of the United States understood the difficulty. They believed that history had given them the opportunity to decide, as Alexander Hamilton wrote in the first Federalist Paper, whether men are indeed capable of basing government on "reflection and choice, or whether they are forever destined to depend . . . on accident and force."

Government by reflection and choice called for a new style of leadership and a new quality of followership. It required leaders to be responsive to popular concerns, and it required followers to be active and informed participants in the process. Democracy does not eliminate emotion from politics; sometimes it fosters demagogy; but it is confident that, as the greatest of democratic leaders put it, you cannot fool all of the people all of the time. It measures leadership by results and retires those who overreach or falter or fail.

It is true that in the long run despots are measured by results too. But they can postpone the day of judgement, sometimes indefinitely, and in the meantime they can do infinite harm. It is also true that democracy is no guarantee of virtue and intelligence in government, for the voice of the people is not necessarily the voice of God. But democracy, by assuring the rights of opposition, offers built-in resistance to the evils inherent in absolutism. As the theologian Reinhold Niebuhr summed it up, "Man's capacity for justice makes democracy possible, but man's inclination to injustice makes democracy necessary."

A second test for leadership is the end for which power is sought. When leaders have as their goal the supremacy of a master race or the promotion of totalitarian revolution or the acquisition and exploitation of colonies or the protection of greed and privilege or the preservation of personal power, it is likely that their leadership will do little to advance the cause of humanity. When their goal is the abolition of slavery, the liberation of women, the enlargement of opportunity for the poor and powerless, the extension of equal rights to racial minorities, the defence of the freedoms of expression and opposition, it is likely that their leadership will increase the sum of human liberty and welfare.

Leaders have done great harm to the world. They have also conferred great benefits. You will find both sorts in this series. Even "good" leaders must be regarded with a certain wariness. Leaders are not demigods; they put on their trousers one leg after another just like ordinary mortals. No leader is infallible, and every leader needs to be reminded of this at regular intervals. Irreverence irritates leaders but is their salvation. Unquestioning submission corrupts leaders and demeans followers. Making a cult of a leader is always a mistake. Fortunately hero worship generates its own antidote. "Every hero," said Emerson, "becomes a bore at last."

The signal benefit the great leaders confer is to embolden the rest of us to live according to our own best selves, to be active, insistent, and resolute in affirming our own sense of things. For great leaders attest to the reality of human freedom against the supposed inevitabilities of history. And they attest to the wisdom and power that may lie within the most unlikely of us, which is why Abraham Lincoln remains the supreme example of great leadership. A great leader, said Emerson, exhibits new possibilities to all humanity. "We feed on genius . . . Great men exist that there may be greater men."

Great leaders, in short, justify themselves by emancipating and empowering their followers. So humanity struggles to master its destiny, remembering with Alexis de Tocqueville: "It is true that around every man a fatal circle is traced beyond which he cannot pass; but within the wide verge of that circle he is powerful and free; as it is with man, so with communities."

ARTHUR M. SCHLESINGER JR.
New York

1

A Prophecy Fulfilled

The brutal close-quarter fighting had been going on since dawn—desperate struggles with hatchet, sword, mace, even bare fists. It was nearly sunset, the bodies of dead French lay strewn everywhere, and still there was no sign of a breakthrough. And now crazy Joan, who had got them into all this, was down. He could see her, not very far off, a great English arrow through her shoulder, her face twisted in pain.

He should have listened to his better judgement. What had ever persuaded them all to follow her? Why, it was preposterous. A mere girl commanding troops? And a girl without a whit of common sense besides. Her behaviour in today's battle showed that: a direct attack on Les Tourelles, the strongest English fort for miles around. Positioning herself right in the front line without a helmet, leaving her neck and shoulders entirely unprotected, just so that, as she put it, her men might see her and take heart? All utterly foolhardy.

No, all she could offer them was this wild, crazy confidence. She was sent by God to lead them to victory, she said. Just be sure you are right with God, attack, and victory will be yours.

Joan of Arc prays for divine guidance. her habit of seeking inspiration from her voices caused particular concern to the judges at her trial in 1431, when she also claimed that the Dauphin and members of his court had had similar mystical experiences.

Joan of Arc rallies her troops during the fighting to raise the siege of Orléans in May 1429. The English, recognizing the strategic importance of Orléans, a major city on the Loire River (which separated the English and French sections of France), had begin the eventually fruitless siege in October 1428.

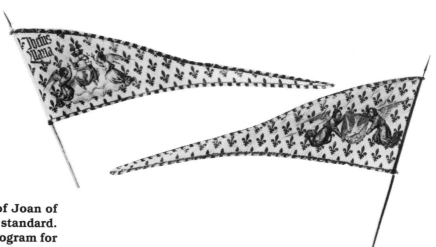

A reconstruction of Joan of Arc's personal standard. The medieval monogram for the Holy Name of Jesus constitutes the inscription. The portrayal of Christ set against a field of lilies (the French emblem) promotes the idea of a sovereign France as the chosen country of God.

And they had believed her. She had asked more of them than any commander he had ever known—and they had done it, willingly. Mass before every battle. No swearing. And here she had them fighting for 12 hours with no sign of permission to retreat.

Yes, they had been fools, he thought to himself. Still, he would not hold it against the girl, especially now that she was suffering. He started over to the spot where he had seen her go down to offer her some of the special salve a gypsy woman had given him. But when he reached it, she was gone. She had removed the arrow herself, a knight told him. Just got up and went off under a tree to pray to her saints.

The soldier laughed bitterly. Now she had really gone too far. Prayers were not going to stop her pain any more than they could produce a French victory today. His mood as black as ever, he turned back towards the fighting. He didn't want to miss the signal for retreat when it came.

But then out of the corner of his eye he caught sight of Joan's banner. It soared as high above the foray as ever, its colourful image of Jesus and the angels streaming in the wind. And it was Joan, with her one good arm, who was carrying it, making her way once again towards the front line.

He could hardly believe the look on her face. Still pale, but on fire—yes, her eyes were on fire. And her voice had the steady strength of one reborn. "In God's name, do not retreat," she called out to the troops. "Fear nothing, attack, and the fort is ours!"

And in that moment he knew it would be as she said. Just hearing her, he could feel a new surge of energy coursing through him. The doubts of the last half hour melted away. Yes, it all seemed mad— this girl and her saints, his readiness to believe in her—but in this crazy confidence lay the greatest hope France had known in nearly 100 years.

The first quarter of the 15th century was a low point for France. A war with England (now called the Hundred Years War) had been raging on and off for decades. The fighting had been entirely on French soil, and the country's villages had been devastated by the constant skirmishing and continual raids by soldiers on both sides.

The people were badly demoralized, and the English were rapidly gaining ground. With the help

Joan of Arc holds up a banner decorated with the *fleur-de-lys* (lily flower), a motif which remains a French national emblem. In Joan's time the symbol was so highly regarded that permission from the king was required for its use.

Philip the Good, duke of Burgundy from 1419 to 1467, first allied with England in 1420, when he recognized Henry VI as heir to the French throne. He gradually withdrew his support as England's position deteriorated after 1429. In 1435 he recognized Charles VII of France, whom Joan of Arc had declared the rightful monarch six years earlier.

of their ally, the duke of Burgundy, they had conquered most of northern France. Even Paris was now under English control.

And just when the French were in need of capable and inspiring leaders, the men on the throne were weak and incompetent. Charles VI was insane. His wife, Queen Isabeau, was little better. She was a loose and irresponsible woman who had frequent affairs with her husband's courtiers and squandered his money on wild parties. The English took full advantage of this situation. Playing on Charles's fear that his son was a bastard, they persuaded him to sign a treaty in which he agreed that the French crown would not pass to his son, as was traditional, but to the son of his daughter instead. Since Charles's daughter was married to the King of England, it was likely that the French crown would one day pass to the King of England.

Charles VII, son of Charles VI, was not mad, but as a leader he was little better than his father. He grew up with a deep sense of inferiority and certainly no sense of kingliness. At an early age he heard the rumours that he was a bastard and not worthy of occupying the throne. There was almost no one at the degenerate royal court to whom the young Charles could turn for love and affection. To make matters worse, he could not rely on good looks or physical prowess to derive a sense of worth. Charles was a truly ugly young man, with a large, bulbous nose, jowls, and drooping eyelids that made him look slow-witted. He had very low blood pressure and thus often felt physically weak. Early on he developed a real fear of physical combat — not a good trait in a future king. In fact, the thought of having to perform on the battlefield terrified him.

Perhaps another man might have challenged the treaty his father had signed and put up a fight for his throne. But Charles VII was far too unsure of himself. He was content to be thought of simply as

Charles VII, king of France between 1422 and 1461. After being a weak leader in the early part of his reign, in 1436 he began a 17-year series of campaigns which would drive the English out of France.

A sword typical of those used by knights throughout Europe during the 15th century. Medieval knights lived by the code of chivalry, which demanded gallantry, honourable behaviour, consideration for the weak, and constant generosity towards enemies.

The *donjon* at Beaugency, where the English garrison took refuge when Joan's forces captured the town in June 1429. A *donjon* was the central tower in any medieval castle.

the Dauphin, the term the French used to refer to the eldest son of the king.

He did make a half-hearted attempt to have himself properly crowned but in the end stood idly by as the English declared the infant Henry VI king of both France and England.

At a time when things looked most hopeless for the French, rumours began to circulate of a prophecy made years earlier by the wizard Merlin. He had predicted that France would one day be ruined by a wanton woman from a foreign land, but then saved by a maid from Lorraine. The first part of his prophecy had already come true. The woman from a foreign land was surely Queen Isabeau. The second part, however, seemed a bit far-fetched. How could a young girl from the farming district of Lorraine save the kingdom of France? Surely a great and noble warrior would be needed to accomplish that. Yet people began to look towards Lorraine and wonder, and perhaps hope.

In 1412 a baby girl named Joan was born in the village of Domrémy, on the border of the province of Lorraine. The girl's family were peasants. Her father, Jacques Darc (later mistakenly written as d'Arc, which translates into English as "of Arc"), owned a house and a little land, and was a minor village notable. Still, despite this bit of security and prestige, life for the Darc family was hard. There was no school for Joan and her sister and three brothers. Instead, they all spent much of their time

Joan of Arc as a child, portrayed by the French painter Virginie Demont-Breton. In a tradition dating back to medieval times, artists have often portrayed female saints tending animals and performing everyday tasks, evoking a holiness defined by simplicity.

The house in which Joan supposedly grew up in Domrémy, France.

helping their parents with work on the family farm.

Yet Joan was a happy child and content with the lot life had dealt her. She was fond of both her parents and especially close to her father. She loved sewing and spinning but also relished being outdoors. She threw herself with gusto into the games and athletic contests popular with the children of the village. To all appearances there was nothing very unusual about Jacques Darc's daughter.

There was one way, however, in which Joan stood apart from the other girls and boys her age. She would never stray from what she believed in her heart to be right and good, no matter what others might say. For example, she did not join in when groups of girls made offerings of flowers to fairies. Instead she would offer some to the saints.

When Joan was 13 this ability to heed her inner voice took on a whole new dimension. Joan had been dancing in her father's garden along with several of her girlfriends. It was noon and she was hot and tired. She had collapsed under a large tree to rest. Suddenly she saw a great light and heard a voice speak to her. Soon she could make out shapes in the light. It was St Michael and several angels. The voice told her to be a good girl and to go to church often.

After that day the voice never left her for long. St Michael spoke to her two and three times a week. Soon Joan heard St Catherine and St Margaret speak to her as well.

At first the counsel of the voices was very general. They continued to advise Joan to lead a good life and attend mass regularly. When she was 16, however, St Michael came to her with a much more specific message. "Go, go, daughter of God, into the realm of France," he commanded. "You must drive out the English and bring the king to be crowned." The village where Joan and her family lived lay within territory partially controlled by the duke of Burgundy,

The village of Domrémy, Joan of Arc's birthplace, in northeastern France. In 1820 the regional government built a triumphal arch at the entrance of her childhood home.

Joan of Arc, portrayed as a maidservant, prepares food for a knight. The artist's conception does not reflect the historical truth, since Joan, of peasant birth, would have had little contact with the nobility.

and was considered outside the realm of France.)

On hearing this, the frightened Joan cried out, "I am but a poor maid and know nothing of war." The voice merely answered, "God will help you." Until now obeying the orders of her voices had not been too difficult. She had to suffer occasional teasing from her friends but that was all. How could she possibly obey such a huge order? Fear welled up in her and she began to cry.

But as Joan thought about St Michael's answer—"God will help you"—a sense of peace came over her, and a deep resolve began to take root.

Joan of Arc is inspired to save France by St Michael, the first of her communicating saints. The evidence concerning the saints of Joan's early visions remains confused. One of her aides testified in 1456 that Joan told him her first saintly visitants were Louis I, emperor of the West from 814 to 840, and his father, Charlemagne.

2
Setting Out

At first Joan did nothing. Her parents would never let her leave. How could she ever explain to them? But the commanding voice came to her more and more often. "Daughter of God, go, go, go, I will come to your aid." So one day Joan simply left. She hated to cause her father grief but she knew she had to follow the voices.

Before setting out for France, the voices had told her she would need to get the backing of the local lord, Robert de Baudricourt, who lived in Vancouleurs, a city not too far from Domrémy. Getting Baudricourt's backing was not easy, however, for Sir Robert was a worldly administrator, not one to put stock in a peasant girl's voices. Yet Joan tried no ploys. She was honest and direct. "It is the will of my Lord that the Dauphin be made king and have the realm in his command. In spite of my enemies he will be king. I myself shall conduct him to his crowning."

"Who is your lord?" Baudricourt asked. "The King of Heaven," Joan answered. At this Baudricourt laughed. He ordered that Joan be taken home to her parents and given a good thrashing.

Joan returned home deeply discouraged and thinking that perhaps she had been a fool to listen to the voices. She wondered if perhaps she should just marry, settle down, and forget this unheard-of sense of mission.

Joan of Arc recognizes the Dauphin, Charles VII, at Chinon on February 25, 1429. The account of Joan's recognizing the Dauphin, despite his attempts to make himself inconspicuous, was written by a lawyer present at the event.

The village church at Domrémy, Joan of Arc's birthplace. The church is dedicated to St. Rémy, patron saint of the city of Rheims, where the kings of France were crowned.

But in the autumn of 1428, events made Joan more keenly aware than ever of her country's need for help. Word had spread that Burgundian armies were preparing to attack Domrémy. The entire village had to flee to a nearby walled town for safety. When the villagers returned they were aghast at the

Joan of Arc as portrayed by 19th-century French painter Jules Bastien-Lepage, who specialized in scenes of peasant life. Joan's image has undergone many transformations since her death, from the warrior maiden esteemed by nationalistic French historians to the innocent yet noble peasant popularized by romantic writers in the 18th and 19th centuries.

brutal way the Burgundians had treated the town. They had even defaced the church. What was happening in Domrémy was being repeated all across France. In October the English laid siege to Orléans, one of the most important cities remaining in the control of France.

Joan was overcome by remorse. How could she have given up so easily? How could she have let her voices and her country down when there was clearly so great a need? She decided to try again to convince Baudricourt of the urgency of her mission.

This time she had to be even more secretive. Her father, in an angry moment, had threatened to

Joan of Arc seeks the approval of Robert de Baudricourt, governor of Vaucouleurs, for her mission to Chinon to see the Dauphin. Joan's seeking the approval of a political figure, rather than that of a bishop, did not help her claim to divine guidance in the eyes of her judges in 1431.

Joan of Arc seeks the approval of Robert de Baudricourt for her mission to see the Dauphin at Chinon. When accused at her trial of having had an affair with de Baudricourt, Joan denied the charge, stating that should she ever have children, they would be fathered by the Holy Spirit.

drown her if she ran off again. But "had I a hundred fathers and a hundred mothers, I still would have gone," Joan later said.

In January 1429 Joan left once again for Vaucouleurs. This time she was determined not to give up. Her voices had been speaking to her more insistently, giving her ever more specific instructions. They told her she was to relieve the siege of Orléans. So even though Robert de Baudricourt sent her word that he would not see her, she did not leave. She found lodgings and settled in at Vaucouleurs. The earnest young girl in red skirt and long black braids was soon a fixture in the town. She told her story to any of the townspeople who would listen, and it was not long before all of Vaucouleurs was taken in by her. They found her modest, intelligent, kind, and—most importantly—not at all mad.

Joan impressed noblemen as well as peasants. One of Sir Robert's squires, Jean de Metz, was so impressed by her that he promised to escort her to the king himself.

Soon talk of the young girl who wanted to save France spread far beyond Vaucouleurs. It reached all the way to the royal castle at Chinon and the ears of the Dauphin himself.

One day a royal messenger arrived for Baudricourt with word that the girl Joan was to proceed at once to Chinon to meet the Dauphin. At last Sir Robert was forced to give her mission his backing.

By this time Joan had become so popular with the townspeople of Vaucouleurs that all she needed from Baudricourt was his official backing. Jean de Metz and two other squires offered to accompany her and pay her expenses. Her cousin Durand and a friend scraped together the money to buy her a horse. Several local ladies made her a page's habit. Others got her boots and spurs. Finally even Sir Robert joined in the enthusiastic send-off. He gave Joan a sword and embraced her when she left.

On the 11-day journey to Chinon Joan's confidence grew. She found she loved the company of these brave men of action who were accompanying her. She felt their equal in spirit and courage. She loved to fool and joke with them. And when dangers arose—which they often did, since the trip to Chinon was mostly through territory held by the English or the Burgundians—it was Joan as often as the others who was able to keep the group from falling prey to panic.

Her companions were awed by her. They had never known anyone like this spirited young girl who loved soldierly exploits yet insisted on going to mass, even in enemy territory.

It was at this time that Joan began to refer to herself as "Joan the Maid". In the 15th century the word "maid" meant "serving girl". Joan had come to identify herself above all with the task of serving: serving her voices, her God, her country, and her king.

Joan of Arc is visited by an angel in her sleep. Some historians believe that Joan's taking on noble dress angered senior French commanders, since they believed that aristocracy was only truly conferred by virtue of noble birth.

VA. VA ... ET ADVIENNE QUE POURRA

Joan of Arc receives her first sword from Robert de Baudricourt in February 1429. De Baudricourt, initially a staunch supporter of Joan and her cause, was later a witness for the prosecution at her trial.

On February 24, 1429, Joan arrived in Chinon. At 8:00 P.M. the following evening the summons came. Joan was to come to the court and meet the Dauphin. Over three hundred people turned out for the event. The castle was packed with richly dressed nobles, festooned with the royal green and white banners, ablaze with the light of hundreds of torches.

Despite her humble background, Joan was not in the least intimidated by the grandeur of the setting. She entered calmly and graciously, her focus on her mission. She had said she would recognize the Dauphin when she saw him. Her eyes scanned the room until something in her commanded her to rest her gaze on a somewhat ugly young man with a large nose and drooping eyes. He did not look at all kingly. But Joan knew. She went up to him and fell on her knees before him. "God give you life, gentle king," she addressed him.

Charles was deeply impressed by Joan's steady conviction. Perhaps this girl would be able to help him as she said. He decided to take her aside and question her further. Could she give him some sign so he would know for sure he could trust her? To this day no one knows exactly what Joan said to Charles. But whatever the nature of the private exchange between the two, when Charles emerged he was radiant. All present agreed that he looked as if he had seen an angel. He had been won over.

On the eve of her triumph Joan urged the Dauphin to hurry and press her into service. She repeated to him what her voices had recently told her: "I will last but a year—scarcely more." But whatever Charles might have wanted to do, he was too weak-willed to go against his advisers. These men, greedy for power and influence, resented the hold this young girl had so quickly gained over the Dauphin. They thought that if it could be shown that her voices and her power did not come from God, but from the Devil, Charles might be persuaded to ignore her.

And so, in mid-March Joan was sent down to the

Joan of Arc before the Dauphin at Chinon. Joan displayed some inconsistency in recounting the event at her trial in 1431, much to the confusion of her judges. At one point she said that an angel had come to the Dauphin, bearing a crown, and that others in the gathering had seen the miracle.

Joan of Arc, equipped as a knight, leaves Vaucouleurs for Chinon and her audience with the Dauphin, in January 1429.

city of Poitiers to be investigated by the learned men of the Church.

Joan consented to the investigation but from the start she was impatient with the scholars and their questions. Although she was unschooled, Joan refused to be intimidated by the churchmen's tricky reasoning. She told them the truth as she saw it, and let her case rest on her simple, direct sincerity. "I know not A from B," she said, "but I come on behalf of the King of Heaven to raise the siege of Orléans (end the British occupation) and lead the king to Rheims for his coronation."

Frequently Joan's candid responses showed up the pettiness of the churchmen's questions. When asked if she believed in God, she answered, "More than you do."

The investigation dragged on for weeks. But at only one point did Joan lose her patience. She had been asked for clear signs that she was from God. "I have not come to Poitiers to make signs," she exclaimed. "Take me to Orléans and I will show you the signs for which I have been sent." And then she went on to spell out, more clearly than she ever had, the "signs" her voices had told her she would make for them. She promised to end the siege of Orléans, to see the Dauphin crowned at Rheims, and to drive the English out of France.

Try as they would, the Poitiers scholars could find no solid ground on which to discredit Joan. And the longer they observed her daily life, the harder it was to maintain any suspicion of this simple peasant girl. In her personal habits, Joan was a model young woman: well-mannered, church-going, sober, moderate. More important, the goodness of her heart was evident to all. She showed great compassion for the city's poor and for its children. The common people loved her.

At last, in mid-April, the churchmen handed down their decision. They pronounced Joan "a good Christian and Catholic".

Joan was elated. The great mission that lay ahead was clearer than ever. Now she was eager to pursue her goals.

Joan of Arc receives the blessing of the churchmen at Poitiers prior to her departure for Orléans in April 1429. Her questioners were members of the Parlement in exile, who fled Paris in 1418 when John the Fearless, duke of Burgundy, occupied the city for the English.

3

The Great Victory

When the king heard the decision made at Poitiers, he at last gave Joan permission to proceed to the cities of Tours and Blois, close to the besieged city of Orléans. She was to prepare for battle with the English troops.

As Joan prepared the troops assigned her for the march on Orléans, they soon saw that this was no ordinary commander. Nor were her sex and age all that made her different. She grew furious whenever she heard the men swearing. She forbade them to pillage and insisted they get rid of the loose women who followed the camp. The soldiers were urged to attend mass every day and to make confession before every battle. To lead her forces into battle she had a special standard made, on which was an image of Christ flanked by two angels.

Joan's men soon came to love her, despite her intolerance of some of their bad habits. In return, Joan truly loved her troops. She revelled in their fooling and boisterousness and telling of tall tales. In fact, nowhere did she feel happier than in the company of soldiers. Joan was good but she was not prissy.

The troops' love for their young commander was

Joan of Arc, in full armour, dedicates herself to the service of her country. The code of chivalry, which demanded Christian conduct and military bravery of knights, was realized in the figure of the crusader, a holy warrior. For his defeat of Satan, many medieval writers saw St Michael, Joan's first saintly visitant, as the first example of a true crusader.

Joan of Arc receives the Sword of St Catherine shortly after arriving at Chinon. According to legend, she had prayed at a shrine to Catherine en route to Chinon and later, commanded by their voices, sent emissaries to the shrine, where they found a sword engraved with the holy words "Jesus" and "Maria".

inspired by more than her affection, however. They had been hungry for someone who could bring out the best of them, and stir them to nobility and valour. It had not been lack of manpower or equipment that had led to their losses to the English, but a simple lack of morale. Now they thrilled to the vision Joan held out to them.

Unfortunately the commanders' response to Joan was not nearly as enthusiastic as was that of the men under her. The thought of letting an 18-year-old girl join their ranks was absurd to them. Even though they had been instructed by the Dauphin "that nothing shall be done without conferring with the Maid", they were very reluctant to grant her such authority. They were also hesitant about making the kind of direct, all-out assault which Joan was insisting on. The English had built seven forts around the city of Orléans. Their position was

Joan of Arc rides at the head of a company of knights. Many nobles in the service of the Dauphin resented the fact that Joan came to enjoy knightly status following the success of her audience with the Dauphin at Chinon.

well-entrenched, and driving them out was bound to be a very costly affair. The commanders preferred to wait a bit longer and see if perhaps the English would weary of the siege and leave of their own accord. Joan might be useful as a mascot who could boost morale, they thought, but as little else. They planned for her to deliver supplies to the people inside the besieged city and to cheer them.

When Joan finally found out what the men in authority had in mind for her, she was furious. One day she had set out with her troops and a load of supplies. They had loaded the supplies onto barges to be floated down the river to the city. When the men assigned to her abruptly turned face and headed back toward Blois, Joan was astonished. Dunois, the leader of the Orléans forces, explained to her that the men had been ordered to do nothing more than deliver the supplies. After all, she would

Joan was pious and she felt great pity at such massacres. Once, when a Frenchman was leading away some English prisoners, he struck one of the Englishmen on the head so hard that he left him for dead. Joan, seeing this, dismounted from her horse. She had the Englishman make his confession, supporting his head and consoling him with all her power.
—LOUIS DE COUTES
Joan's page, at rehabilitation trial

The statue of Joan of Arc at Chinon, executed by the sculptor Jules-Pierre Roulleau in 1893. According to one of her followers, Jean d'Alençon, Joan displayed great skill on horseback.

Joan of Arc falls from a scaling ladder during fighting to raise the siege of Orléans in May 1429. While Joan was injured in battle, she swore at her trial that she had never killed anyone. The historical evidence indicates that she acted more as figurehead than field commander.

not need men to boost the morale of the Orléans citizens. And right now, he continued, a morale boost was what was wanted.

Joan would not be calmed. She would have none of Dunois's arguments for caution and patience. "The advice of our Lord is wiser and more certain than yours," she warned him. "You thought to deceive me, but it is you who are deceived." She insisted he recall her men or she would leave. Dunois was not normally a man to be easily swayed. But there was something about Joan's sureness of purpose he could not resist. He recalled her troops and on April 29 they entered the city of Orléans.

Once inside she found the commanders still reluctant to let her attack. They were outnumbered, they told her, and it was far too risky. Joan would not listen. Her voices were growing more insistent than ever. With God on her side, there was no reason to worry, she urged.

On the morning of May 4 Joan was awakened early by a great commotion in the street. It turned out that the French forces had attacked the small English fort of Saint-Loup without telling Joan. She was furious to realize that the commanders were still so obviously distrustful of her. But she wasted little time on her anger. She quickly had her page help her into her armour, mounted her horse, took her standard and sword, and sped off to the scene of the battle.

When she reached Saint-Loup, fighting had already been going on for some time. As usual, the French were weakening seriously. But when the men caught sight of Joan's standard, they rallied. Within a few hours it was all over. The French had taken their first English fort in many months.

The day after the Saint-Loup victory the army council assembled to draw up plans for their next move. Joan was not invited, as she should have been according to the Dauphin's instructions, but she showed up anyway and let them have a piece of her mind. "You want to hide your intentions from me? Well, I won't tell you what I intend to do either. But you'll see it, you'll be aware of it soon enough. You and your council. I have my own counsel

Joan of Arc prays in the chapel of the Virgin Mary at Vaucouleurs. The cult of the Virgin Mary, Mother of God, was prominent during the 14th century, creating a religious awareness in France which fostered many prophecies of a virgin saving the country.

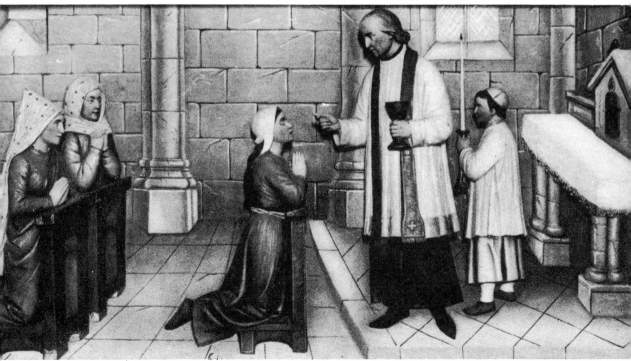

Joan of Arc removes an arrow from her shoulder at the siege of Orléans in May 1429. Joan's persistence in continuing the fight despite her injury demoralized the English.

(meaning her voices) and it is a good deal better than yours!"

On May 6 Joan rose before dawn and ordered her page to blow his bugle. By daybreak she was already in her armour and mounted. The people of Orléans quickly rallied to her standard. In the short week Joan had been among them they had been completely won over by her. They had none of the commanders' caution, and Joan's valiant call to arms captured their hearts.

Although the governor of Orléans refused to open the city gate for Joan, the mob soon prised off its huge lock and streamed through the gate behind their adopted leader.

Joan's plan was to take two of the smaller English forts which surrounded Orléans. Then, with the

Joan of Arc at the siege of Orléans in May 1429. The most important aspect of Joan's military usefulness was her ability to inspire bravery in others.

English badly shaken, she would assault their major stronghold, the fort of Les Tourelles. Her strategy was simple: no diversions, just direct attack. When the French reached the first fort, Saint-Jean-Le-Blanc, the English, awed by this new French audacity, gave it up almost on sight. The second fort, Les Augustins, had been steadily built on the ruins of an old monastery and would not be so easy. Yet by nightfall the English had surrendered this one as well.

Despite this magnificant showing, when the commanders heard Joan announce that the next morning she planned to proceed with the attack on

Joan of Arc encourages her troops at the siege of Orléans. The French victory greatly aided Joan in her effort to convince people that God was guiding her.

The battle rages at the siege of Orléans. Joan's seemingly miraculous successes during the battle earned her the gratitude of the French and the fearful admiration of the English.

Les Tourelles, they urged her to rest instead. Her men were tired, they pleaded. A 15th-century battle was a bloody, intense, and exhausting affair. Since guns had not yet been invented, most of the fighting was at very close range. The chief weapons were bow and arrow, lance, and sword. The storming of a fort or city involved considerable hand-to-hand combat. Scaling ladders were laid against the walls and the men battled it out at the top. A few hours of this was all most troops could endure.

Despite her troops' weariness Joan would not swerve from her plan. The morning of May 7 she was again up before dawn and attending mass. With colourful banners flying, the tired but confident army set out for Les Tourelles. When they reached the fort the men threw themselves into the assault. Observers were amazed at their fury. But Les Tourelles was an especially well-designed fort. A

French troops shelter in temporary forts as their artillery opens fire on an English bastion during the siege of Orléans.

deep ditch around its base made its walls extremely difficult to scale. By late afternoon many French had fallen and still little headway had been made. Then Joan, who had been in the front line all along, was felled by an arrow in her left shoulder. This deeply disheartened her men. But as soon as her wound was dressed, she retired to a quiet spot in a nearby meadow to pray. "I am going to ask God about the attack," she told them.

In just a quarter of an hour she had returned. They should make one more attempt, she insisted. And although still weak and dizzy from her wound, she raised her standard high with her good arm and yelled at her troops to charge.

When the men saw Joan's standard a new wave of energy and resolve swept through them. They stormed the towers of the fort with a fresh fierceness. This time they were too much for the English, who began fleeing across the Loire River outside the fort by means of a hastily mended drawbridge. But the French had not only recovered their energy. They had regained their wits as well. They had loaded a barge with pitch, tar, and oily rags, ignited its cargo, and floated it down under the bridge. Soon the bridge's planks caught fire and over 20 British soldiers, including their leader, Glensdale, plummeted into the Loire. Weighed down by their armour (at least 23 kilograms' worth per man), they plunged to the river bottom and to their deaths. Les Tourelles was taken.

The next morning, May 8, Joan received word that the English had decided to abandon even the forts that remained theirs. The captains asked Joan whether they should pursue them, but she answered, "Let them go. God does not will that we fight this day." She had already shed many tears for the English dead. Orléans was French again. That was all that mattered.

In just three days Joan had accomplished what the army commanders had insisted could not be done at all. The people of Orléans believed that they had witnessed a miracle, and their awe and gratitude knew no bounds. Every church bell in the city was set ringing. People poured into the streets singing hymns of thanksgiving. The city's priests organized processions in Joan's honour, and the authorities declared that from then on May 8 should be a citywide day of feasting. The people treated Joan like a saint. Crowds followed her everywhere, eager to touch her clothes or have her bless their religious medallions.

Soon word of the girl soldier and her amazing powers spread far beyond Orléans. Requests came from nobles all over Europe who wanted Joan's help with every manner of problem. She was showered with gifts: splendid robes, a new suit of armour, fine wine, magnificent horses. Joan took great pleasure in all these things (she especially loved fine clothes and good horses). She saw no conflict between worshipping God and enjoying the material world He had made.

> When 1914 came, the Marne saw triumph those virtues gleaned from the banks of the Meuse (Joan's birthplace). Here it was that our army had reinforced its valour and its patriotic fervour, in order to carry on once again the work of Joan of Arc.
>
> —GENERAL FERDINAND FOCH
> leading French field commander
> during World War I

From just two quarters were the reactions to Joan's triumph less than enthusiastic. The British, of course, were far from pleased. They had been badly shaken by this sudden reversal and were both resentful and fearful of the Maid who seemed to be the cause of it all. In the letter he wrote to the king of England summing up what had happened at Orléans, the duke of Bedford, English governor of Paris, described Joan as "a disciple and limb of the Fiend". On hearing of Joan's exploits, many Englishmen who had been drafted to fight in France refused to go.

More surprising was the lukewarm reaction from the Dauphin. He was certainly not displeased. It seems he rewarded Joan with a good sum of money, and he invited her to visit him at his castle. Yet

Joan of Arc enters the city of Orléans at the head of her army on April 29, 1429. According to Dunois, half-brother of the duke of Orléans, only when Joan took charge of the crossing of the Loire River did the wind change, allowing the French to ferry men and equipment to the city.

Joan of Arc enters Orléans on April 29, 1429. Many citizens of Orléans greeted Joan on her arrival since word of her mission reached the city before she did.

when he wrote a letter to the cities of his realm sending news of the great victory, he mentioned Joan only at the end, almost as an aside. Credit went to the armies and their commanders. And when Joan began to press Charles to let her proceed with the next step of her mission, leading him to Rheims to see him crowned, he stalled and urged her patience. There was something about this young girl that made him uneasy. Her sureness of purpose and largeness of heart, so much the opposite of his own cowardly and self-protective nature, threatened him.

47

4

A True King at Last

Despite his uneasiness, Charles finally decided he would once more entrust himself to Joan's care. She had promised to see him crowned, and this was something he wanted badly.

Before Charles could proceed, however, more battles would have to be fought. The English still held much of the territory through which he would have to pass to get from his Loire valley castles to Rheims. Joan, eager for action, was more than happy to be given this mission. She set out at once.

Her men, however, were not so confident. They knew that the famed commander Fastolf was on his way with reinforcements for the English, and they were scared. But once again Joan's own sureness of purpose quickly lessened their fear. Her voices were clear, and she was sure victory was now within their grasp. "Have no doubt, the hour is at hand when it is pleasing to God," she reassured her troops. "Act and God will act."

Once again her prophecy proved correct. Within little over a week, the French had four stunning victories to their credit. Two of the best of the English commanders, the earl of Suffolk and Lord Talbot, had been taken prisoner. In one battle, at

A superb example of 15th-century armour for man and horse. Many nobles under Joan of Arc's command would have fought thus protected, despite the fact that by this time bows and arrows were sufficiently powerful to pierce all but the very heaviest armour.

Joan of Arc attends King Charles VII of France at his coronation in Rheims on July 17, 1429. Since Rheims was in the part of France occupied by English and Burgundian troops, Charles' journey there was a combination of royal procession and military advance.

Patay, nearly 3000 of Falstof's crack troops were taken. Throughout it all Joan was in the front line risking injury and death with the best of her men.

Unfortunately, routing the English was not all it would take to guarantee the Dauphin a safe trip to Rheims. They would still have to contend with the hostile Burgundians who controlled much of the area around that city.

When it came to dealing with the duke of Burgundy, Charles decided he had had enough of Joan and her noble campaigns. Charles had a strong dislike of battles to begin with. His boyhood sense of incompetence with the sword and lance had never left him. And since 15th-century monarchs were much more closely involved in warfare than are modern day rulers, Charles tried to keep the battles waged in his name to a minimum.

Now Charles's general battle-shyness was compounded by the fact that he had long felt deeply intimidated by the duke of Burgundy, who was his cousin. Duke Philip was supremely self-confident

Joan of Arc (left, in armour) unhorses Lord Talbot at the Battle of Patay on June 18, 1429. According to popular legend, the French lost only three men at Patay, while the English suffered 3,000 casualties.

Joan of Arc chooses her standard-bearer in June 1429.
Historians remain uncertain as to whether Charles VII
ever actually awarded Joan a knight's coat of arms.

and he seemed to have everything Charles lacked. He had a passion for women (by the age of 30 he had fathered 19 bastard children); he had money and style (life at his court was considered the most splendid spectacle in all Europe); and most important, he had ruthless ambition. Unlike the timid Dauphin, Philip had made it clear he was eager to rule as much of France as he could. Charles was deeply afraid of confronting this awesome cousin in any way. He ordered Joan on no account to challenge the duke.

Fortunately, popular feeling had been rising for the man who would soon be king. Even those in the region controlled by Duke Philip had grown excited at the prospect that France would again have a properly crowned monarch at the helm. Their hostility toward Charles melted in the face of rising good feelings, and so the Dauphin met with very little resistance as he passed through the Burgundian territory.

The castle of Mehun-sur-Yevre, where Charles VII was proclaimed king of France in 1422.

When Charles entered Rheims on July 15, the air was jubilant. Everywhere people were already crying out "*Noel! Noel!*" (the ancient way of saying "Long live the King!"). To the common people, as to Joan, a properly crowned king was a gift from God. When a man was consecrated he made a solemn pledge to serve his people as God's deputy. The authority to give orders was then given him by God. This authority was to be exercised with humility for the good of the people entrusted to his care.

For a king to be properly crowned, and for this transfer of power to be effective, the French believed the ceremony had to take place in Rheims. Rheims was where Clovis, the first Christian king of France, had been crowned by St. Rémy in 496.

To show the importance a coronation had in their eyes, the French spared no expense on the ceremony. This one began at 9:00 A.M. July 17, a Sunday morning. The entire town and many visiting nobles turned out. The cathedral was a riot of shimmering colour, the brilliant hues and gold threads of the nobles' robes playing off against the rich deep purple of the priests' cassocks and the glistening jewels on their gloves.

Joan of Arc dedicates the Sword of St Catherine to the
service of France in 1429. Joan's claim that her voices
had told her where to find the sword greatly disturbed
the judges at her trial in 1431.

The coronation of Charles VII of France at Rheims on July 17, 1429. Due to the wartime conditions the ceremony was less splendid than on previous occasions.

Charles swore with his hand on the Bible to defend the Church and preserve his people and govern them with justice and mercy. Then a deep blue cape decorated with the lilies that were a symbol of the French royal house was draped over his shoulders. All was sealed when the archbishop dipped his finger in the holy oil and made the sign of the cross on Charles's forehead.

Throughout it all Joan stayed close by Charles, her attention wholly focused on the man who was now her king. Despite her key role in bringing about this event, she was humbly dressed in a simple suit of plain armour. She did not want to steal the show. Her standard, however, she carried proudly aloft. It stood out as the only military standard in the ceremony. But to Joan this much display was fitting, for in her eyes the standard did not point to her, but to the God she served, the God who stood behind all the miracles of the last three months.

The archbishop of Rheims anoints Charles VII of France with holy oil on July 17, 1429.

5

Dark Clouds Gather

The coronation was a moment of great triumph for both Joan and Charles. The Maid had accomplished the second task her voices had set for her. Her great faith and persistence had been grandly rewarded. For Charles. his lifelong dream to be recognized as a true king had at last come true.

After the ceremony the city of Rheims erupted in celebrations and merrymaking. Joan was besieged with requests to be godmother. Letters of congratulations poured into Charles from all over the realm. As signs of their new loyalty several cities offered him the keys to their gates. Even some of the cities in the territory controlled by the duke of Burgundy made friendly overtures to the new king.

Yet these two who had captured the hearts of France reacted very differently to the groundswell of public favour. Joan saw this as the ideal time to press on to the third task her voices had set for her: the liberation of the rest of France, and especially of Paris, from English and Burgundian control. Clearly the country was in a mood to rally behind such a campaign. So shortly after the coronation Joan began to press Charles for permission to move on Paris.

Charles was a fearful and small-minded man,

Joan of Arc sees saints bringing her a sword and banner. During her early days as a champion of Charles VII, Joan claimed that two French heroes, Louis I and Charlemagne, had appeared in her first vision. Joan's later citing of St Michael shows an inconsistency which greatly confuses historians.

CHARLES VII ROY DE FRANCE

Charles VII of France (1403-1461). His signing of the Edict of Compiègne on August 29, 1429, greatly angered Joan, since it allowed a four-month truce between France and Burgundy at a time when Charles might have achieved more military victories.

The happiness which Joan had felt upon arriving at Chinon and seeing Charles VII (portrayed here in a 15th-century German tapestry) became despair several months later when Charles signed a treaty with the duke of Burgundy, suspending the French struggle against England.

more concerned with assuring his personal safety and comfort than in furthering the interests of his kingdom. He had always been a bit reluctant to follow the Maid, and had been driven to open-mindedness only by his desperate situation.

But now that he enjoyed some power and prestige, his true colours began to show. Rather than head north and proceed with the campaign to restore the rest of his kingdom, he meandered south. There he could relax and enjoy the leisurely life at court safe in the territory he already controlled. Any sympathy he had once had for Joan's military enthusiasm had vanished entirely.

In this battle-weary and lethargic mood, Charles was more vulnerable than ever to the influence of his crafty advisers. These men had long been jealous of the favour Charles had shown the young girl from Domrémy. But now they saw a chance to get the king to turn away from Joan and rely on them instead. They promised to settle things with Burgundy through negotiation rather than on the battlefield. Within just days of the coronation they had a preliminary treaty in their hands, and by mid-August a four-month agreement.

Joan had already been annoyed by the king's retreat to the south. But when she heard the terms of the treaties her annoyance deepened to outrage. By signing them it seemed to her that Charles had just bartered away the very thing they had been fighting for: the chance to reunite all France under

Joan of Arc communicates with her saints. The fact that Joan's voices continued to urge her to carry on fighting the English after Charles VII had suspended hostilities proved fateful in September 1429, when her unsuccessful assault on Paris damaged her reputation for invincibility.

a single ruler. Charles had granted Burgundy the right to remain independent of him. He had also agreed to return to Duke Philip many of the cities that had recently come over to his side.

Joan also suspected that Burgundy would not uphold his end of the ceasefire. It was rumoured that just before negotiating the treaty with Charles, he had completed another with the English in which he arranged for 3,500 reinforcements to be sent him.

Joan's sense of duty to her king could barely restrain her. She expressed her outrage to Charles directly: "Truces so fashioned do not make me happy," she told him. "Nor," she added, "am I sure I shall observe them."

When Joan's warnings got no response she grew deeply disheartened. She fell prey to dark moods, and on several occasions lost her temper in a way she never had before. One day she erupted in a fury at the camp women who travelled with her soldiers,

The coronation of Charles VII of France at Rheims on July 17, 1429. Three days after the ceremony Charles fulfilled a traditional duty of French monarchs in medieval times when he went to touch the holy relics of St Marcoul at Corbény. The act was supposed to give the king healing powers.

chased one of them clear out of the camp, and hit her with a sword with such force that it broke.

Not only was Joan angered and disheartened by the treaties. They also caused her to feel a strange foreboding about her future. Something in the treaties made her suspect that those who had made them would not long tolerate anyone, such as herself, who dared point out how bad these agreements were for France. When asked if she were never afraid. Joan replied, "There is only one thing I fear, and that is treachery."

At one point she came near to giving up. "Would that it please God," she exclaimed, "that I might now withdraw, foresake arms, and return home to serve my father and mother in herding their sheep."

Her voices, however, were insistent and unwavering. "Go, daughter of God, go, go, go!" they told her.

Yet there was one clause in the second treaty which gave Joan heart: both sides agreed that the

Joan of Arc at the siege of Orléans in 1429. While greatly contributing to the final victory, Joan's inspired leadership at Orléans disturbed some French commanders, who thought that her love of independent action showed a lack of professionalism.

city of Paris would be exempt from the ceasefire. Doubtless Burgundy had agreed to this because he felt there was no longer any chance that the French could take the city once fresh British troops arrived. But as for Joan, so long as the possibility of attack was there, she felt hopeful.

She began to press Charles more insistently than ever to let her proceed to Paris. The king was still very hesitant to let her go, but at last gave in and allowed her and her old friend, the duke d'Alençon, to prepare. She would have to raise her own troops, however. Royal support for the campaign would be minimal.

This indifference about taking Paris puzzled Joan. Why had the king agreed to the clause that exempted Paris from the ceasefire unless he was interested in trying to take it? But she wasted little time over this mystery and proceeded with her battle preparations with her usual gusto.

The first week in September Joan and d'Alençon prepared to assault the city from two sides. D'Alençon built a makeshift bridge over the Seine River on Paris's south side. But on the first day of the attack they concentrated all their forces on the north side. The fighting went very poorly. Joan saw her own page killed before her eyes. She herself was badly wounded by an arrow in the thigh. By nightfall even Joan was ready to retreat.

She insisted on resuming the assault first thing the next morning, however. Yet she and her men had scarcely got into position when two messengers approached her with orders from the king to cease fighting. Joan was furious. How could Charles give up that easily? Didn't he care about the most important city in the land? No, she and her men would simply change their tactics and attack from the south.

But when she reached the spot from which she and d'Alençon had planned to launch their southern assault, she discovered that their makeshift bridge had been burned during the night. And it was neither Englishmen nor Burgundians who had burned it, she was told, but the king's men.

Now she understood the strange feelings of fore-

You Englishmen, who have no right in this Kingdom of France, the King of Heaven orders and commands you through me, Joan the Maid, that you quit your fortresses and return into your own country, or if not I shall make such mayhem that the memory of it will be perpetual.
—JOAN OF ARC
in a letter to the
English commander at Orléans

boding that had plagued her in the last weeks. Treachery was indeed to be feared—and at the hands of the king himself. Charles had not truly wanted to take Paris. No wonder he had been so lukewarm about her plans for the attack. He and his crafty advisers merely wanted to give Joan a chance to fight in a situation in which they felt sure she could not win. Perhaps a defeat for the Maid would lessen her great influence with the people, would cut support for her aggressive campaign. No doubt Charles had felt confident that the enemy would take care of it for him, but he had not been above undercutting his own men to ensure it.

In a mood of near despair, Joan ordered her men

The statue of Joan of Arc at her childhood home in Domrémy, France. The many statues of Joan throughout her country attest to her continuing importance as a symbol of French nationalism.

Joan of Arc, *Pucelle* of Orléans, as portrayed by Louis Foucault in 1674. *Pucelle* is an old French word which means virgin.

to retreat. Then she went off alone to the abbey of Saint Denis, a short distance outside Paris, and prayed.

As the autumn wore on, the king's desire to undermine Joan became increasingly clear. At the end of September he disbanded the fine and staunchly loyal group of knights who had been with her since the siege of Orléans. They were sent to various locations in the north. Joan was not allowed to go with them.

To keep her busy and out of the way while he pursued his negotiations, Charles assigned the Maid to put down rebellions in two towns along the Loire River. These were particularly difficult assignments. Again, it seemed Charles was eager to see Joan defeated.

The king tried to cover up his subtly hostile actions by welcoming Joan to stay in his various chateaux. He also raised her to the ranks of the nobility and gave her the new last name "de Lys". (Only nobles were allowed to use last names that began with "de".) But these gestures did little to raise Joan's spirits. She felt more like a prisoner in the castles than like a guest. She never used her new last name. Now only the chance to honour her voices and fulfil her mission could bring her true happiness.

Joan of Arc astride her charger. Since Joan chose to fulfil her mission as a knight, in accordance with the tradition of chivalry, some historians suspect that as a child she must have been told stories concerned with chivalrous deeds and exploits.

Captain La Hire and Poton de Xantrailles, two of Joan's senior aides on the Orléans campaign in 1429. The two men were more military adventurers than ideal knights, often engaging in sheer banditry under the pretext of fighting for Charles VII of France.

By the spring of 1430 Joan's impatience was acute. The previous March, while at Poitiers, her voices had told her she would last "only a year—scarcely more". And nearly a year had passed since then. Her time was running out. Her sense of urgency about resuming the campaign against the English and the Burgundians was heightened by rumours that Duke Philip was planning a major offensive for the spring.

By the end of March she could bear her inaction no longer. Without telling Charles, she decided to round up whatever freelances (men who fought for whomever would pay them) she could and set off on her own. She paid them herself, out of the money she had received from Charles after the victory at Orléans.

On her way north Joan stopped in the city of Melun to celebrate Holy Week. She spent much time in prayer and listened closely to her voices. Their message for her was far from pleasant. "You will be captured before St. John's Day," they told her. (St.

John's Day was June 24.) At first Joan was frightened. The prospect of a long captivity and possible torture terrified her. But her voices reassured ˌher that God would help her to bear whatever happened to her. Soon she was calm again. There was no turning back. She could only go forward and trust.

Her first destination was the city of Compiègne, an important town that was considered the gateway to the north. The duke of Burgundy had been attempting to occupy Compiègne. Weak-willed Charles had simply advised its citizens to surrender to the duke. But the city would have none of the king's submissiveness. They wanted to resist and they urged Joan to help them.

By nightfall of May 22 Joan had arrived at Compiègne. The following morning she and her men rode through the city's gates, over the great drawbridge that spanned its moat, and on to the Burgundian camp.

But the Burgundians had spotted them moments after they had set out, and had quickly sent for reinforcements. By the time the French arrived the Burgundians were more than ready for them. Joan's freelance soldiers soon realized they were overwhelmed. Despite the Maid's valiant efforts to rally them, a wave of panic spread through her troops. She decided she had no choice but to order a retreat. As always Joan stationed herself in the place of greatest danger. In attack she had always been in the front line. Now, in retreat, she brought up the rear.

As the retreating French drew near to Compiègne, they scrambled across the drawbridge to the safety of the city walls. But by the time Joan reached them, the drawbridge had been raised. The city's governor had felt the enemy were too close to leave it down any longer. For the sake of his citizens' safety the few French that remained outside would have to be sacrificed.

Soon Joan found herself completely surrounded by Burgundians. One of them caught hold of the long robe she was wearing over her armour and pulled her from her horse. Joan knew it was all

The castle at Sully-sur-Loire where Joan stayed in March 1430 prior to her final campaigns.

over. She had known it was coming, and now gave herself up to it. She surrendered quietly to the first knight that approached her and allowed herself to be taken back to the Burgundian camp.

Within two days word of Joan's capture had

Joan of Arc is taken prisoner at Compiègne on May 23, 1430. Although Charles VII made no attempt to ransom her, he did threaten to harm English prisoners unless Joan's captors treated her well.

spread all over France. The nation was deeply upset.
It was the custom then for any prisoner of high
rank to be held for ransom. Letters poured in to the
king begging him to pay whatever price was asked
to free the young girl who had done so much to

defeat the British and restore their national pride.

But the letters seem to fall on deaf ears. The reaction of the court was far different than that of the common people. One of Charles's advisers went so far as to say that Joan had deserved her fate: "God suffered that Joan the Maid be taken because she had puffed herself up with pride and because of the rich garments which she had adopted."

Charles himself made no comment. Nor did he make any move to negotiate for Joan's release as his subjects had urged. He was too much under the sway of his advisers, and his desire to keep out of trouble with Philip had by now almost completely suppressed any feelings of gratitude or indebtedness he felt toward the young girl who had gained him his crown.

But if the king of France was uninterested in ransoming Joan, others were. Chief among these, of course, were the English.

The English were exultant at the news of the capture. Charles's efforts to discredit Joan and destroy her reputation for special power, wisdom, and inspiration had had no effect whatsoever on his enemies. If anything, their fear of Joan, their conviction that she possessed supernatural powers, and their urge to do away with her had grown.

There was another group which also had a keen interest in Joan: the Church. Actually, it had had its eye on her for some time. This was the age of the Inquisition, a time when the Church felt increasingly threatened by the growing numbers of people who defied its authority or disagreed with its teachings. The Pope had appointed special judges, called Inquisitors, to try such people for heresy. (Heresy was the crime of believing something contrary to the beliefs of the Church.) A convicted heretic might be subject to severe punishment or death.

Early in her career, the theologians at the University of Paris had begun to see Joan as a threat. These churchmen had played a key role in drawing up the treaty in which Charles VI had agreed to pass his crown to the son of the English king, and thus turn France over to English rule. It was they who

Any book about Joan which begins by describing her as a beauty may be at once classed as a romance. Not one of Joan's comrades, in village, court, or camp, even when they were straining themselves to please the king by praising her, ever claimed that she was pretty.
—GEORGE BERNARD SHAW

had provided the theological defence for this document, which overturned all commonly accepted beliefs about how the kingship could be passed on.

Joan's campaign had showed up the hollowness of their clever arguments, and so they were as eager as were the English to do away with Joan. The day after they got word that the Maid had been captured, they sent a letter requesting that Joan be turned over to the Inquisitor in Paris for trial as a heretic.

Actually, these two groups, the English and the Church, were far from being rivals in the bidding

Joan of Arc is led before her Burgundian captors in May 1430. Pierre Cauchon, the pro-English French bishop who eventually ransomed her, hoped that by disproving Joan's claim to divine guidance he would be able to undermine Charles VII's position as monarch of France.

A miniature from *The Champion of Women* by Martin le Franc, portraying Joan as comparable to the biblical heroine Judith, who slew the tyrant Holofernes and was often used by medieval writers as the prime example of the great virtue of Fortitude.

for the captured Maid. The English were gleeful at the prospect that the woman they had accused of sorcery might be officially tried and found guilty of heresy. In their thirst for vengeance, such a conviction seemed almost important to them as the chance to do away with Joan. And the churchmen were quite sympathetic to the English. Paris, after all, had been controlled by the English for several decades.

All it took was a clever negotiator to get two groups to agree to share in determining Joan's fate. The man who arranged the fateful agreement between the two parties was an ambitious bishop named Pierre Cauchon. By the terms of this agreement, the English would pay Joan's ransom (the kingly sum of 10,000 francs), but would then turn her over to the Church authorities to be tried. Yet in so doing the English would not sacrifice their role in determining Joan's fate, for the Church had agreed to hold the trial in a way that allowed the

Joan of Arc as portrayed by the 17th-century artist Jean de Caumont. The text at lower right praises Joan as an "Amazon" of France. (The Amazons, according to Greek mythology, were a race of warlike women fully as capable in battle as men.)

She was the pioneer of rational dressing for women.
—GEORGE BERNARD SHAW

A statue of Joan of Arc as a perfect knight, in armour and bearing a sword. The submissive pose suggests the humility which popular belief has accorded her.

The tower of the castle of Rouen, France, where Joan was imprisoned in 1431.

greatest possible English influence and thus the greatest possible chance of the guilty verdict they so wanted. It would be held in Rouen, the most strongly English city in France, rather than in Paris as was customary. And in the unlikely event that Joan was found not guilty, Cauchon had got the Church to agree to return her to the English.

For this ingenious deal Cauchon was rewarded handsomely by both sides. The English paid him well for his efforts, and the Church officials in Paris gave him permission to be the chief presiding judge at the trial.

While negotiations for her ransom were going on Joan was locked up in the castle of Beaurevoir, under the watch of the Burgundian John of Luxemburg. Despite the fact that she was now a prisoner, her sense that she had a mission remained as strong as ever. After a time several of the women of the court took pity on her and offered to have a dress made for her out of especially fine fabric. Joan thanked them, deeply touched by their kindness, but turned them down. She would continue to wear her fighting man's clothes, she said, as a sign of her dedication to God. She did not feel at liberty to wear anything else until her voices let her know her mission was over.

Joan was unable to see how her imprisonment could possibly further the cause of her king and her country, or be a part of the mission God had set for her. Still, she submitted. She trusted the goodness of God's plan, and her voices, which were with her every day now. The graciousness with which Joan conducted herself at Beaurevoir amazed her captors.

Late in November she was told that she had at last been sold to the English and would soon be turned over to them and tried as a heretic by the Church. From the moment she arrived in Rouen Joan sensed that she would be facing by far the most difficult test of her faith.

Joan had every confidence that she would be found innocent. She knew she was no heretic, no rebel against God. And she knew that any honest judge could see how much she loved her Lord and how wholeheartedly she strove to serve him.

But it was also clear to Joan that hers would be anything but an impartial trial. She was being kept in a squalid prison cell in the English castle at

Joan of Arc receives the instructions of her saints. Joan found herself increasingly addressed by her voices during her captivity.

Joan of Arc has a vision of her saints. Joan, like many medieval visionaries, only maintained widespread popular approval for as long as her prophecies came true.

Rouen. She knew Church law normally granted the accused the right to be quartered in a Church prison (generally far more comfortable and humane than the prison of any government). If the English had been able to twist this much of Church law, what else might they be able to do?

During the winter, as she waited in her cold cell for the proceedings to begin, Joan turned again and again to her voices for councel and comfort. Without her saints, she could not possibly face what was ahead. But they assured her over and over that she would receive help so long as she was true to them. "You will be freed by a great victory", St. Catherine told her. Joan did not know what this meant but she trusted her voices.

6

The Maid on Trial

She had seen the room where her trial was to take place, and it was forbidding. Her two judges, Bishop Cauchon and the Inquisitor of Paris, were to be seated in huge, high-backed chairs, flanked by dozens of priests, called assessors, who would act as a kind of jury. Many of these, as citizens of Rouen, were sympathetic to the English cause and would want revenge. The accused would face this imposing group seated on a small, lone footstool, designed to make her feel all the more keenly her lowliness and isolation.

Yet, firm in her dedication to her saints, Joan was able to enter and take her seat radiating strength and composure. As soon as the proceedings began, on February 21, 1431, this strength was put to the test.

The first order of business was the administration of the oath of truthfulness. This was a routine procedure to the judges, but not so for Joan. It called into question the whole matter of where her first loyalty lay. "Concerning most matters," said Joan, "I will willingly swear. But the revelations made to me by God, I have not told nor revealed to anybody excepting only to Charles, my king, and I shall not reveal them though it cost me my head. I have been told that by my visions and by my secret councel, to reveal them to nobody." Cauchon pressed her for hours but she held firm. "I have a

Joan of Arc as she appeared on the day of her burning, May 30, 1431.

Joan of Arc as portrayed in a 16th-century manuscript. Joan's more critical biographers point out that her career as a knight was far from perfect according to the conventions of chivalry. She conducted her final campaign as a "freelance", a status generally associated with banditry and adventurism.

greater fear of being at fault by saying something which displeases these voices than I have of not answering you," she told him. Finally the bishop was forced to let the matter drop.

As the trial proceeded, the spectators were awed by the way Joan handled the steady bombardment of questions. The questions came at her from all directions, one after another. They were subtle and designed to trip her up. Yet Joan refused to be intimidated. Her voices councelled her to "answer boldly". She held to their advice.

Not only was she truthful and straightforward, but occasionally bold enough to puncture her questioners' air of sombre self-importance with a bit of wit or sarcasm. When asked if St Michael had appeared to her naked, she replied, "Do you think God could not afford to dress him?" On another day the bishop asked her if there had been light when she greeted the Dauphin. "Yes," she answered, "for all light does not emanate from you, monsignor."

Without deliberately trying to be evasive, Joan

Joan of Arc appears before Bishop Cauchon in February 1431. Cauchon was a brilliant churchman and politician who maintained close ties with both the English and the duke of Burgundy. He amassed a vast fortune in the course of his devious career.

Joan of Arc is brought to trial in 1431. Her chief prosecutor, the pro-English Bishop Cauchon, sought to prove that Joan's voices were not divine and that Joan's recognition of Charles as rightful monarch of France had thus been inspired by the Devil.

A reconstruction of the mitre which her prosecutors forced Joan to wear when she was burned at the stake. The text describes her as heretical, relapsed, apostate (deserter from faith), and idolater (one who worships a false god).

managed to avoid being caught in the many legalistic traps her judges and assessors set for her. One of their trickiest questions was, "Do you know if you are in God's grace?" If she said she was, she would be found at fault for claiming to know something which only God could know. Yet if she answered in the negative, she would leave herself open to charges that she was an agent of the Devil. But Joan avoided both dangers. "If I am not," she answered, "may God bring me to it; if I am, may God keep me in it."

Many of those who listened to Joan felt that not even the learned men who were questioning her could have answered so well.

The proceedings continued for six weeks, with three to four hours of questioning each morning, and often two to three hours after the midday meal as well. At first the assessors pursued what seemed like dozens of different lines of questioning. They were eager to find as many possible grounds for conviction as they could. But most proved unfruitful. It was difficult to prove conclusively, as they attempted, that Joan was a witch, a sorcerer, or a murderer.

Eventually, however, the judges and assessors found a focus for their prosecution: her stubborn refusal to submit completely to their authority. At the time of the Inquisition, even the slightest refusal to submit in any way to the authority of the Church's bishops was grounds for conviction as a heretic. According to the theology of the time, the officials of the Church were thought to receive power and inspiration directly from God in order to win souls for him. So to love and obey God implied loving and obeying the Church and its officials.

Evidence that Joan placed loyalty to God and her voices above loyalty to the Church began to mount from the very first day of the trial. It was first seen in her refusal to swear to reveal all that her voices had told her.

Next it arose over the issue of Joan's dress. She was appearing for trial in the page boy's garb she had worn since she left for Chinon. For a woman to wear man's clothes was a crime against God, the judges told her, and they cited a passage from the Bible to prove their point. They ordered Joan to put on a woman's dress but she refused. Her voices had not yet told her to change costume, and it was their command she would wait for. "These clothes do not burden my soul," she said. "As for woman's clothing, I shall not put it on until it please God."

Joan's insubordination came to a head with her refusal to accept the court's judgement that her voices were evil, that they originated with the Devil. It was the duty of an untrained person, they maintained, to submit any visions or voices to the judgement of the Church, and then to abide by its decisions. Only a Church official, inspired by God, could determine the origin of such voices.

When the churchmen decided to focus their attention on her voices, it was not difficult to credit

Joan appears before her judges in February 1431. A major charge against Joan was that she had failed in her religious duty by not seeking the advice of a churchman upon first experiencing her revelations.

them. The teachings of the day concerning voices
and visions made it especially easy. These doctrines
held that voices that came from God were seldom
concrete. It was the Devil, rather, who produced
voices and visions that were specific. Such seeming
reality was just another sly way the Fiend had of
misleading people. When Joan was asked questions
about what her saints looked like, sounded like,
even smelled like, she was, unfortunately for her
case, able to supply details. She could not do
otherwise and remain truthful. Few things were so
real to her as her saints.

Repeatedly the judges insisted that she admit her
voices were of the Devil. This Joan simply could not
do. "Everything good I have done, I did by command
of the voices," she protested. It was her voices'
council that had made her a good Catholic. Yet to
prove to these men that she was a true believer she
had to renounce the voices. The idea was ludicrous
to her.

*Joan got a far fairer trial from
the Church and the Inquisition
than any prisoner of her type
and in her situation gets
nowadays in any official
secular court.*
—GEORGE BERNARD SHAW

Joan told them over and over of her love for the
Church and its teachings, of her fervent desire for
confession and the chance to receive communion.
But this was not enough.

"Do you not believe that you owe submission to
God's Church on earth, that is, to our Lord the
Pope, to the cardinals, archbishops, and other
prelates of the Church?"

"Yes," Joan answered, "but God must be served
first." For Joan, that "but" was critical. To eliminate it would be to deny all that she was and knew.
"You shall have no other answer," she told them. In
the eyes of her judges, however, only a simple "yes"
would do. To this central question, "yes, but" was
the answer of a heretic.

By the beginning of April the judges and assessors were satisfied that their case against Joan was
a strong one. They drew up a dozen formal charges
and extracts from Joan's testimony which they
believed supported them. These they read before
the entire court assembly on April 12. No matter
that the evidence for most of the charges was flimsy
(in many cases so weak that her assessors had been
forced to twist much of what Joan had said in order

Joan of Arc is led into captivity at Rouen in December 1430. The detail is taken from a manuscript published in France during the 16th century.

to make it at all believable). There was one charge that was serious enough to make up for all the others: "She will not submit herself to the determination of the Church militant (the Church on earth), but to God only."

The reading of the charges was far from the end of the trial, however. Since this was a Church trial, the charging was not immediately followed by sentencing and punishment, as in a civil court. Instead, a court of the Inquisition followed with a series of procedures designed to help the accused see and admit his guilt, and renounce his error. This was done because Church courts were concerned with saving souls, rather than simply seeing that justice was done. If a person renounced his error, he could be pardoned, readmitted to the folds of the Church, and his soul spared the fires of damnation. Therefore that part of a trial during which various procedures were used to get the accused to "recant" (renounce his mistaken ways or beliefs) was an important and often lengthy one.

The original inspiration for this part of the trial was that of compassion. However, this had been badly distorted as the Inquisition progressed. Many of the procedures used in the name of saving souls were the ruthless pressure tactics and ghoulish tortures for which the Inquisition is best known. And so the month that followed the charging, the month in which Cauchon and his associates attempted to save Joan's soul by bringing her to repentance, proved to be the most horrible the Maid had yet had to endure.

Joan was already in a poor state. Despite her heroic performance in the courtroom, she had been seriously weakened by the long weeks of questioning. To make matters worse, she had been subjected to ill treatment of all sorts from the moment she arrived in Rouen. In her prison cell she was chained to her cot, and often ridiculed and treated crudely by her English jailers. She was not even allowed the consolation of her religion. So long as she continued to wear man's clothes, her captors declared, she could not receive communion or even set foot in a church. One of her guards was seriously punished for taking pity on his prisoner and allowing her to pause in prayer at the entrance to a chapel.

As a result of this shabby and degrading treatment, Joan had fallen seriously ill. She was feverish and vomited frequently. She could not move from her cot.

Yet despite her low state, Cauchon insisted on carrying on with the next phase of the trial. He and several associates went daily to Joan's cell, where they spent hours trying to wring from the exhausted girl an admission that her voices were evil.

Joan was pale, drawn, and utterly weary. Perhaps she should simply give in. Could God, could her saints, possibly want her to go on like this? But the very voices she was being asked to declare false and evil seemed closer to her than ever. They were one source of comfort, and they assured her over and over that God would save her, so long as she put all her trust in him. How could she possibly go against her saints, in whom she had put her trust for so long? No, she would not, could not, recant.

By the first week in May the churchmen were getting impatient. They decided to increase the pressure. One morning Cauchon led Joan to the castle's torture chamber. There, surrounded by boots with screws that could be tightened until her ankle bones broke, by irons that could be used to

The only surviving tower of the castle of Beaurevoir, where Joan was imprisoned during July and August 1430.

The earliest surviving image of Joan of Arc, drawn by a government clerk when he recorded the raising of the siege of Orléans in the register of the Paris Parlement in 1429.

sear her flesh and melt her eyeballs, they put their question to her again. Did she still maintain that her voices were of God, that she answered first to God rather than to the Church?

Joan remained as firm as ever: "Should you tear my limbs from me and drive my soul from my body, I could tell you nothing else." There was something about the steely defiance in her voice that unnerved the bishop. It quickly became clear to him that torture would do nothing to bring the resolute, stubborn young girl to repentance. The plan was abandoned.

Joan did at last allow that there was one church-man to whose judgement she would submit—the Pope. If the court would let her go and plead her case before him, she would abide by his decision. But Cauchon was too shrewd to grant such a request (this despite the fact that Church law entitled her to such a hearing). He no doubt sensed, as did Joan, that a less partial judge such as the Pope would find her innocent.

More important, this was *his* trial, *his* chance to show what he could do. And he had not yet exhausted his bag of tricks. Although physical torture might not shake Joan, perhaps something more subtle and psychological would.

Joan knew that both her saints—Margaret and Catherine—had been martyrs, had been put to death for refusing to renounce their faith. Despite her tremendous courage, the thought that a similar fate might await her was almost more than she could bear. She had an especially deep dread of death and fire. She had pleaded with her voices many times to reassure her that she would not end up being burned at the stake.

Cauchon was well aware of this vulnerability in Joan. So on Thursday, May 24, he arranged for her to witness a scene that would play on her one great fear. In the cemetery of Saint-Ouen, just outside the city walls, he had a scaffold and two wooden platforms erected amid the grey and weathered gravestones. Stationed prominently near one of the platforms was an executioner's cart. Everything about the dreary site called to mind the fate that awaited Joan if she did not recant.

Early in the morning Joan was driven out to Saint-Ouen. Assembled on one of the platforms were Cauchon and the rest of the assessors. Joan was led up onto the smaller platform, alone except for a guard and a priest. From there she looked out on a sea of unsympathetic faces.

The priest then began to preach to her a long, stern sermon. He went over and over the vileness, the lowness of her many offences. He talked of her great evil and pride. He spoke of the great ill she had done her country and her king. Again and again he pressed her to recant. "Will you revoke all your sayings and deeds which are reproved by the judges?" he asked her.

Joan's answer remained the same as ever: "I abide by God and our Holy Father the Pope." This was not good enough. Three times the priest repeated his question. Still Joan held fast.

The priest paused. Then he took out the paper on which was written the formal sentence that con-

The tower of the castle at Rouen, where Joan's inquisitors threatened her with torture in 1431.

A 16th-century miniature portraying Joan of Arc set against a field of lilies (the emblem of French royalty) and standing on a dais which displays the names of Jesus and the Virgin Mary. Such imagery promotes Joan as a national and religious heroine.

demned Joan to be turned over to the civil authorities and burned. Slowly he began to read.

When these solemn, final words reached them,
many of the assessors watching Joan from the
larger platform could no longer contain themselves.
No matter what their prejudices, when at last it hit
them what would be the fate of the young girl
opposite them, they begged Joan to submit and

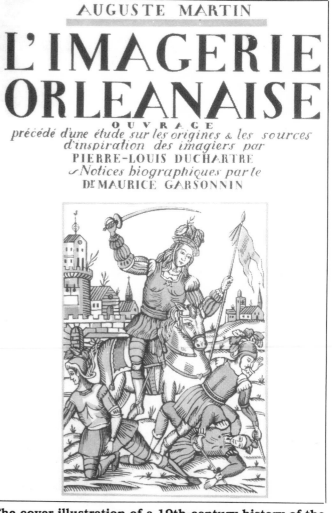

AUGUSTE MARTIN

L'IMAGERIE ORLEANAISE

OUVRAGE
*précédé d'une étude sur les origines & les sources
d'inspiration des imagiers par*
PIERRE-LOUIS DUCHARTRE
Notices biographiques par le
D' MAURICE GARSONNIN

The cover illustration of a 19th-century history of the
imagery surrounding Joan of Arc. After Joan's death, a
vast diversity of images evolved according to the
political, spiritual, and moral standpoints of those
seeking to preserve her memory.

**Joan of Arc listens to her
voices. The statue, by
Henri Chapu (1833-1891),
stands in the Louvre Mu-
seum in Paris.**

save herself from a terrible death while there was yet time.

Their pleas mingled with the whooping of the rowdy Englishmen in the crowd, who were excited

Joan of Arc as portrayed by the British artist Dante Gabriel Rossetti (1828-1882).

by the prospect of a public burning of a heretic.

Amid all the clamour one word stood out for Joan: "fire". Cauchon's tactics had succeeded at last. This was too much for her. Suddenly she called for the priest to stop reading. She had changed her mind, she said. She would renounce her voices, put on woman's clothes, and do whatever else the churchmen told her.

The crowd was stunned. Abruptly its mood changed. The Englishmen, realizing they had just been cheated of the burning they had lusted for, began to jeer and hurl stones at the platform where Joan stood.

But the judges in charge remained calm. This was just what they had been hoping for, and they had come prepared. They quickly pulled out a prepared statement of recantation for Joan to sign. Its terms included an agreement to put on woman's clothes, and to submit to life imprisonment as a penance for her sins.

Great waves of long pent-up emotion seemed to flow from Joan as she listened to the droning words. As she reached for the pen she shook and gave out an eerie, hysterical laugh. But then she began to breathe deeply again. Calm returned.

Joan of Arc testifies at her trial in May 1431. After Joan's death the chief prosecutor, Cauchon, persuaded Henry VI of England to pardon all the members of the trial court, even though no accusations of wrongful conduct had been forthcoming. Cauchon's move demonstrates the uncertainty the judges felt in their final sentencing of Joan.

Joan of Arc signs the statement of recantation on May 24, 1431. A few days later she confessed not just that fear of burning had made her do so, but that further guidance from her voices had influenced her.

These things she could accept—the dress, a Church prison. At least the horrible ordeal at the hands of the English would come to an end.

But Joan's sense of relief was abruptly dashed, for according to the agreement Cauchon had made with the English back in November, the Church had to hand Joan back to the English if she were not convicted. And the bishop was certainly going to keep his part of the bargain. After all, the English had done him a great favour. Thanks to them he now had one of the most impressive trials in years to his credit.

"Take her back where you brought her from," he commanded the guards. There would be no comfortable Church prison for this penitent. Church law guaranteed housing in its own prisons to a confessed and repentant heretic. But Cauchon's court, under pressure from the British, chose to flout Church law yet again. The guards seized Joan and led her back to the castle they had brought her from just a few hours earlier.

7

The Stake and Afterwards

Despite the momentous events of the morning, little seemed to have changed. Joan's cell was as cold and dank as ever. Once again heavy iron chains weighed down her ankles. Only one thing was different. Joan's page garb had been stuffed into a bag and tossed carelessly into the corner. In its place she had been given a long dress to wear.

For several days Joan sat in her cell listless and despondent. She stirred herself only to fend off the lewd approaches of her guards, which seemed worse than ever. At one point she asked if she might be allowed to hear mass. But even this comfort, which she yearned for with all her soul, was still to be denied her.

Joan's spirits sank lower than ever. The prospect of the life ahead dismayed her greatly: years, decades of this same dreary cell, of chains and abusive guards. And on top of it all, still no chance to hear mass. But even these things she might have endured, were it not for a growing torment deep in her soul.

For relief Joan turned, with more earnestness than ever, to the one source of comfort that remained to her: her voices. Yet what they seemed to be saying was hardly comforting. At first she

> *In her is found no evil, but only good, humility, chastity, devoutness, honesty, simplicity.*
> —verdict of Poitiers examiners

Joan of Arc as portrayed by the French artist Jean Ingres (1780-1867).

Joan of Arc in her prison
cell, chained to a bed of
damp straw, is interrogated
by the Bishop of Winches-
ter.

could scarcely bring herself to listen to them.

But her saints were like a conscience that could
not be quieted. They were gentle, but insistent. You
did not do well last Thursday, they told her. Your
horror of the stake is understandable, but you let
your fear of fire cloud your judgement. You served
neither God nor the truth with what you said. You
spoke only to save your life, and by doing so you
have damned yourself.

It did not take long before Joan knew what she
had to do. There was only one way to regain any
sense of comfort within herself. She would once
again have to tell the truth. She would have to
withdraw her recantation.

Joan knew well what this meant. Anyone who

repented of heresy but then returned to the old ways was considered a relapsed heretic—the worst kind. Only the harshest sentence could be passed on a relapsed heretic, and that meant death by fire. In the eyes of the Church, nothing less would suffice. But Joan's old strength had returned. Once again her priorities were clear. Nothing, not even life itself, mattered to her so much as that feeling of being true to herself, true to her voices and her beloved God.

She retrieved the rumpled pile of men's clothes from the corner where the guards had heaped them. She might as well put them on. She knew she had been expressly forbidden to wear them. The minute anyone caught sight of her once again in her page's outfit, she knew the authorities would be notified. But what did that matter now? She would have to confront them sooner or later. And in the

The burning of Joan of Arc on May 30, 1431. Isambart de la Pierre, a priest who attended Joan during her last hours, claimed that an English soldier saw a dove (symbolizing the Holy Spirit) flying from French territory as Joan died.

meantime her old clothes symbolized her reborn faith and strengthened it. She put them on.

Before the day was out Cauchon and several of the others had descended on her cell. Joan trembled as she looked into their stern and merciless faces. Tears came to her eyes. Cauchon bellowed "Why have you assumed this male attire and who made you take it?" Joan answered, "I have taken it of my own will."

She paused, still fearful, but then regained her composure and went right to the heart of the matter. "All I have done these last few days I did for fear of the fire, and my revocation was against the truth. I have never done anything against God and against the faith, whatever I may have been made to revoke." With that Joan set in motion a fatal chain of events from which there was no turning back.

The following morning a friar was sent to inform the prisoner of the sentence that had been passed on her and to administer last rites. Joan let out a great moan when she heard the news. "Ah, I had rather be seven times beheaded than to be burned," she wailed.

Many writers have compared Joan's death to Christ's crucifixion. Alexandre Dumas, the 19th-century novelist, went so far as to call Joan "the Christ of France".

The death of Joan of Arc has inspired many French poets, even into the 20th century. René Char, a highly unconventional poet, published a poem in 1956 which attempted to penetrate the mystery of Joan of Arc's unique sanctity.

But after making her confession and receiving communion, a certain peace came over her. It would sustain her through the awesome rituals of the next few hours: the donning of an old dress dipped in sulphur (to help it to catch fire more quickly), the lonely ride out to the town square in the executioner's cart, the first view of the scaffold with the sticks piled high around its bases, the masses of hostile English, the dozens of churchmen solemnly arrayed on a dais. Even through the lengthy sermon that was preached to her, she remained serene and composed.

Then Bishop Cauchon began to read the final sentence, in which he declared that Joan was a relapsed heretic and thus must be turned over to the civil authorities to be dealt with accordingly.

Due to its doctrine of mercy, the Church was not allowed to inflict punishment. However, a convenient arrangement had been worked out with civil authorities over the years in which the courts of the

> *Lying, Evil, Unbelieving,*
> *Cruel, Dissolute*
> —sign at base of scaffold
> on which Joan of Arc was burned

Many writers who admire Joan of Arc have viewed her death as sacrificial. The French poet Lamartine (1790-1869) considered Joan's fate "complete" by reason of her martyrdom for faith and country.

**A 19th-century drawing of
the statue of Joan of Arc in
Orléans. The sculptor, Gois
(d. 1836), portrayed Joan as
a Republican, in costume
from the period of the
French Revolution.**

Inquisition convicted and recommended certain
punishments, and the civil justice system had them
carried out.

With the reading of the sentence the solemn,
plodding pace of the proceedings immediately
picked up, and the seething emotions that had
been held in check for hours broke loose. Joan
began to pray aloud, and with tears and great
passion called on God and the saints. She begged
over and over for the crowd to forgive her, to pray for
her, and promised in turn to forgive them.

Soon much of the assembly was also in tears,
including many of the churchmen who had conde-
mned her. Even the English were deeply moved.
When Joan asked for a crucifix, it was an English

Joan of Arc as portrayed by painter Albert Lynch. Although Joan never received royal approval for decorating her banner with the *fleur-de-lys*, it is interesting to note that Charles VII granted her family the name "du Lys" when he ennobled them in 1429.

soldier who rushed to lash two sticks together and hand them to her.

Joan took this makeshift cross and stuffed it into the front of her dress. Again an unearthly calm came over her. Then quietly, with dignity, she mounted the great pile of wood and sticks at the base of the scaffold. She stood still as the executioner bound her to the pole. She had just one last request. Would someone go into the church, get the crucifix, bind it to a long stick, and hold it close by her face so that she might have the comfort of gazing on it during her last moments? One of the churchmen sped off to do her bidding.

The flames rose quickly. As they neared the sulphur-soaked robe Joan began to call out. For several minutes all that could be heard in the hushed square were the crackling of the flames and the piercing cries of a young girl: "Jesus, Jesus, Jesus." And then, just the spitting of the fire, and it was all over.

In that last moment the full force and significance of Joan's character was felt as it had been at no other time in her life. And with that horrid death a certain power was unleashed in the world that was to go far beyond anything Joan achieved in her lifetime.

The greatness of Joan of Arc lay in her willingness to place loyalty to that which was deepest and truest in her above all else, above what others thought of her or said of her, even above life itself. It was this blazing integrity that had inspired her men and that had given rise to the great accomplishments of her lifetime—the liberation of Orléans, the crowning of the king.

When the world began to see the truly extraordinary measure of that integrity, saw that it would remain unshaken right to her death, Joan's ability to inspire and influence became greater than ever.

Among the people of France, the feelings of loyalty to king and country that Joan had awakened while she lived were only deepened by the news of her tragic end. Their desire to rid their land once and for all of foreign control soon became stronger than ever.

The English were as greatly moved by the spectacle of Joan's death as were the French, but not at all

Joan of Arc as she is often remembered—fighting at the siege of Orléans.

Charles VII enters Rouen on October 26, 1449. French forces had regained the city in 1448, thus crushing the last English hopes of holding Normandy and retaining their sovereignty in France.

in the way they had expected. Rather than feeling jubilant, most came away from the Old Market Square of Rouen deeply unnerved. What had they done, sending to her death a girl who in her last moments could say "I forgive you!" and even call on *them*, her executioners, to forgive *her*? "We are all lost," said one Englishman. "We have burned a saint." From that time on, the proud assurance that had been the source of so many English triumphs in France gradually began to erode.

And so, within 25 years of the burning at Rouen the English were almost completely routed from France, their holdings reduced from close to half its territory to just two cities. The third of Joan's missions had been nearly fulfilled. And in a way the Maid had been almost as much a part of this triumph as she had of the victory at Orléans or the crowning at Rheims.

Joan's death also had a notable influence on King Charles. The young girl who believed in him may not have had the effect she wished during her lifetime. Her influence did not seem equal to that of the king's crafty advisers. But in the years after her burning Charles gradually grew into the sort of king Joan had always believed he could be.

He tempered his indulgent lifestyle and became a serious, hard-working monarch. He chose his advisers more carefully, including several of the knights who had been closest to Joan. With their help he built France into a strong, unified nation. This king who had seemed so fearful and unpromising when Joan knew him was later nicknamed "Charles the Victorious" and "Charles the Well-Advised" by historians.

And there is good reason to suppose that memories of Joan had been much with Charles during these years of transformation. Try as he might, it seemed he could not forget this girl to whom he owed his crown and his kingdom. In fact his consciousness of his debt to Joan clearly grew with the years. He began, quietly but earnestly, to seek out a way to atone for the ungratefulness of his youth.

As soon as the city of Rouen had been won from the English and the records of Joan's trial made available to him, he began to work to get the trial declared invalid and so clear Joan's name. (The

Joan of Arc's mother, Isabelle Romée, kneels before the papal commissioners at Notre Dame Cathedral in Paris on November 7, 1455. The commissioners declared Joan's sentence null and void, but said nothing regarding the issue of Joan's holiness and divine inspiration.

Joan of Arc is surrounded by her communicating saints at her burning on May 30, 1431. Such portrayals of Joan's death promote the legend that to the very end she remained faithful to her voices.

grounds for invalidation would be interference by the English.) It took several years before he was successful, but he persevered.

At last, in 1455, he arranged for a retrial to be held. Witnesses from all over were heard: friends and family from Domrémy, participants in the original trial at Rouen, several of Joan's closest fighting companions. This time the churchmen conducting it were scrupulous. And in 1456 Pope

Calixtus III declared Joan's name forever cleared of all charges against it.

But Joan's special power to influence did not stop with those who had known her. The story of her life and the death that was its inevitable tragic outcome has continued to have a powerful effect on people to the present day.

Joan has been the inspiration for some of the world's greatest artists and writers. And the appeal of her story has not been limited to Frenchmen. One of the greatest plays by English dramatist George Bernard Shaw was based on Joan's life. Joan was also a favourite of American humourist Mark Twain.

Even more important, perhaps, than the inspiration Joan has provided for works of art has been the way in which her story has repeatedly inspired people from all walks of life to remain true to the voice of God within themselves. She has been a special favourite of those who have felt called to tasks that were difficult or dangerous.

Two of the greatest French military and political figures of this century, Marshal Pétain and Charles de Gaulle, had a special devotion to Joan. Russian cosmonaut Komarov, who died on one of his space flights, was reading the story of Joan of Arc when his life ended.

People of many different convictions have found in Joan the inspiration to live up to them more fully. In particular she has fired the souls of French nationalists and Catholics.

If anything, the attraction and power of Joan's story has grown with the passing of time. She was canonized a saint by the Roman Catholic Church, not in the 15th century, but in the 20th (1920)—largely in response to the swelling popular devotion to her.

Thousands of people still turn to Joan's story daily, from the soldier of whom great bravery is required to the young girl who needs the quiet courage to be honest with her lover. In this brief but so-powerful life they find the help they need to remain true, through whatever arises, to the voice within them.

> *She worked with a will, watchful over feeding the animals, willingly caring for animals of her father's house, span, and did the housework . . . She was very devout towards God and the Blessed Virgin, so much so that I myself, who was young then, and other young men, teased her.*
>
> —COLIN
> a childhood friend, at Joan
> of Arc's rehabilitation trial

Joan of Arc on horseback,
as portrayed by the British
artist William Blake Rich-
mond (1842-1921).

Further Reading

Boutet de Monvel, Maurice. *Joan of Arc.* New York: Viking, 1980.

Leary, Francis. *The Golden Longing.* New York: Charles Scribner's Sons, 1959.

Pernoud, Regine. *Joan of Arc: By Herself and Her Witnesses* (translated by Edward Hyams). New York: Stein and Day, 1966.

Shaw, George Bernard. *Saint Joan: a Chronicle Play in Six Scenes and an Epilogue.* New York: Dodd, Mead & Co., 1930.

Williams, Jay. *Joan of Arc.* New York: American Heritage Publishing Co., Inc., 1963.

Chronology

1412	Born Joan Darc in Domrémy, France
1425	First hears voices
1428	Commanded by voices to go to the Dauphin
May 1428	Fails to gain the backing of Robert de Baudricourt for her mission to see the Dauphin
Oct. 1428	Domrémy evacuated due to Burgundian attack Siege of Orléans begins
Jan. 1429	Gains support for mission from Robert de Baudricourt
Feb. 1429	Meets the Dauphin
March 1429	Gains the approval of examining churchmen at Poitiers
April 29, 1429	Enters Orléans
May 4–7 1429	Battle of Orléans
May 8, 1429	Siege of Orléans raised English troops retreat north of the Loire River
June 11–17 1429	Leads French armies to victory at Jargeau, Meung, Beaugency, and Patay
July 17, 1429	Coronation of Charles VII of France at Rheims
Aug. 3, 1429	Charles VII signs truce with Burgundy
Aug. 16, 1429	Charles VII signs second truce with Burgundy
Sept. 8, 1429	French forces fail to take Paris Joan of Arc's influence begins to decline
Nov. 1429	Joan of Arc leads raiding parties against Anglo-Burgundian forces at La-Charité-sur-Loire and Saint-Pierre-Les-Moutiers
Dec. 1429	Joan of Arc ennobled by Charles VII
May 23, 1430	Joan of Arc captured by Burgundian forces at Compiègne and imprisoned in Beaurevoir castle
Nov. 21, 1430	Joan of Arc delivered into the custody of the English
Dec. 23, 1430	Joan of Arc arrives in Rouen
Feb. 21, 1431	Trial for heresy begins
April 12, 1431	Joan of Arc hears the charges against her
May 9, 1431	Threatened with torture
May 24, 1431	Recants at cemetery of Saint-Ouen
May 28, 1431	Withdraws recantation
May 30, 1431	Burned at the stake
1456	Pope Calixtus III declares 1431 verdict against Joan of Arc null and void
1920	Roman Catholic Church admits Joan of Arc to the catalogue of saints

Index

Alençon, Jean d', 38, 62
Amazons, 73
aristocracy *see* nobility
Augustins, Les, 42

Bastien-Lepage, Jules, 26
Beaugency, 18
Beaurevoir, 75, 76, 86
Bedford, duke of *see* John of Lancaster
Burgundy, 26, 49, 50, 52, 59, 60, 62, 66, 67, 71
    see also Charles VII; Compiègne; Joan of Arc;
        Philip the Good
Burgundy, Duke of *see* Philip the Good

Calixtus III, 106
Cauchon, Pierre, 71, 72, 75, 79-81, 85, 88, 92,
    93, 98, 100
    see also Joan of Arc, trial of
Champion of Women, The, 72
Chapu, Henri, 90
Char, René, 99
Charlemagne, 23, 57
    see also Joan of Arc, voices
Charles VI, ("Charles the Mad"), 16, 70
Charles VII, 16-17, 25, 28, 30-31, 46-47, 49-52,
    54, 55, 57-60, 62-70, 104-105
    see also Compiègne, Edict of; Rheims
Chartier, Alain, 17
Chinon, 25, 28, 30, 31, 35, 38, 58
chivalry, 18, 35, 65
Churchill, Winston, 57
Clovis, 52
Compiègne, 67-68
Compiègne, Edict of, 57-62

Darc, Jacques, 18
Dauphin, *see* Charles VII
De Baudricourt, Robert, 25, 27, 28, 30
    see also Joan of Arc, trial
De Caumont, Jean, 73
De Coutes, Louis, 37
De Gaulle, Charles, 107
De Metz, Jean, 28
De La Pierre, Isambart, 97
De La Pole, William (Suffolk, earl of), 49
De Xantrailles, Poton, 66
    see also Orléans
Demont-Breton, Virginie, 19
divine right, 52
Domrémy, 18, 20, 21, 25-27, 63
    see also Burgundy

donjon, 18
Dumas, Alexandre, 98
Dunois, Jean, 37-38, 46
    see also Orléans

England, 13, 15, 16, 21, 27, 33, 44, 46, 49, 57,
    60, 66, 70, 72, 75-77, 79, 93, 103-106

Fastolf, John, 49-50
fleur-de-lys, 15
Foch, Ferdinand, 45
Foucault, Louis, 64
France, 13, 15-16, 18, 21, 25-27, 33, 39, 49,
    52, 54, 55, 57, 59-60, 63, 70, 75, 89,
    103-105
French nationalism, 63

Henry VI, 18, 92
heresy, 70, 82, 84, 93, 97, 100
    see also Joan of Arc, martyrdom; Joan of Arc,
    trial
Hundred Years War, 13, 15, 21, 27, 33, 35-47,
    49-50, 59, 62, 66, 70, 104

Ingres, Jean, 95
Inquisition, 70, 79, 82, 85, 88, 90, 93, 97,
    100-101
    see also heresy; Joan of Arc, martyrdom
Isabeau, 16, 18

Joan of Arc
    canonization, 96, 107
    capture and imprisonment by Burgundians,
        67-75
    Charles VII, association with, 30, 31, 46-47,
        49, 58, 59, 62-65
    childhood, 18-23
    De Baudricourt, first meeting with, 25
    ennoblement, 65, 102
    martyrdom, 79, 82, 96-98, 100-104, 106
    nobility, conflict with, 36-39
    Orléans, Battle of, 13-15, 35, 47, 61
    Paris, unsuccessful attack on, 59, 62-64
    ransomed by the English, 72-76
    recantation, 88-93
        withdrawal of, 95-98
    standard, 14, 35, 51, 102
    Sword of St. Catherine, 35, 53
    treaty with Burgundy, reaction to, 57-62
    trial, 13, 27, 28, 30, 31, 53, 79-87, 92, 96

Vaucouleurs, 28
verdict, reversal of, 105-107
voices, 13, 21, 23, 25, 28, 31, 33, 35, 53, 59, 61, 66, 76, 77, 83-84, 93, 95-96, 106
John of Lancaster (Bedford, duke of), 46
John of Luxemburg, 75
John the Fearless, 33
Judith, 72

knight, 18, 36, 65, 79
Komarov, Vladimir, 107

La Hire, Captain, 66
Ladvenu, Martin, 102
Lamartine, Alphonse, 100
Le Franc, Martin, 72
Loire River, 13
Louis I, 23, 57
    see also Joan of Arc, voices
Lynch, Albert, 102
Mehun-sur-Yevre, 52
Melun, 66
Merlin, 18

nobility, 22, 29, 36
Normandy, 104

Orléans, 40, 101, 103
    Battle of, 13-15, 35-47, 61, 87
    siege of, 27, 28, 32-33

Paris, 16, 57, 59, 62-64, 72, 75
Paris, University of, 70
Patay, Battle of, 50
peasantry, 22
Pétain, Henri Philippe, 107

Philip the Good (Burgundy, duke of), 16, 21, 49, 50, 52, 58, 60, 62, 66, 67
Poitiers, 32-33, 66

Rheims, 25, 32, 33, 49, 52, 54, 55, 57, 60
Roman Catholic Church, 70-72, 75, 77, 82, 84, 85, 87, 93, 97, 107
Romée, Isabelle, 105
Rossetti, Dante Gabriel, 91
Rouen, 75-77, 79, 85, 88, 96, 104, 105
Roulleau, Jules-Pierre, 38

St Catherine, 21, 88
    see also Joan of Arc, voices; Joan of Arc, martyrdom
Saint Denis, abbey of, 64
Saint-Jean-Le-Blanc, fort of, 42
Saint-Loup, fort of, 38, 39
St Marcoul at Corbény, 60
St Margaret, 21, 88
    see also Joan of Arc, voices
St Michael, 21, 23, 35, 57
    see also Joan of Arc, voices
Saint-Ouen, 88
St Rémy, 25, 52
Shaw, George Bernard, 70, 74, 84, 107
Suffolk, earl of see De La Pole, William
Sully-sur-Loire, 67
Sword of St Catherine, 35, 53

Talbot, John, 49, 50
Tourelles, Les, 13, 42-45
Twain, Mark, 13, 49, 107

Vaucouleurs, 25, 28
Virgin Mary, 39